CACA DOLCE

ALSO BY CHELSEA MARTIN

Everything Was Fine Until Whatever

The Really Funny Thing About Apathy

Even Though I Don't Miss You

Mickey

CACA DOLCE

ESSAYS FROM A LOWBROW LIFE

Chelsea Martin

Soft Skull  New York

This is a work of nonfiction. However, some names and identifying details of individuals have been changed to protect their privacy, correspondence has been shortened for clarity, and dialogue has been reconstructed from memory.

CACA DOLCE

First Soft Skull edition: August 2017

"Goth Ryan" first appeared in *Hobart*; "I Lost a Tooth at Work" in *Buzzfeed*; and "Voluntary Responses to Involuntary Sensations" in *Catapult*.

Library of Congress Control Number: 2016952067

Library of Congress Cataloging-in-Publication Data
Names: Martin, Chelsea, 1986– author.
Title: Caca dolce : essays from a lowbrow life / Chelsea Martin.
Description: New York : Soft Skull Press, [2017]
Identifiers: LCCN 2017009907 (print) | LCCN 2017019518 (ebook) | ISBN 9781593766825 (ebook) | ISBN 9781593766771 (pbk.)
Subjects: LCSH: Martin, Chelsea, 1986– | Authors, American—21st century—Biography. | Artists—United States—Biography.
Classification: LCC PS3613.A77783 (ebook) | LCC PS3613.A77783 Z46 2017 (print) | DDC 813/.6 [B] —dc23
LC record available at https://lccn.loc.gov/2017009907

Published by Soft Skull Press
1140 Broadway, Suite 704
New York, NY 10001
www.softskull.com

Soft Skull titles are distributed to the trade by
Publishers Group West
Phone: 866-400-5351

Printed in the United States of America
1 3 5 7 9 10 8 6 4 2

For Ian

CONTENTS

CACA DOLCE

A VERY SPECIAL INTRODUCTION THAT KNOWS IT'S NOT ACTUALLY SPECIAL

Many times when I was growing up, my nana would pull me into her bedroom, close the door behind us, and press a five-dollar bill into my palm.

"Don't tell anyone," she would whisper, referring to, I supposed, my cousins, who were the only people who would possibly have been interested in the transaction, and who were usually playing in the next room. I agreed not to tell anyone because I loved and respected my nana, and because I didn't want to share the money with anyone, and, most important, because I would never have told my cousins in the first place. It would have hurt their feelings.

"You're my favorite," she would often say. "You're the baby."

It was a strange thing to say, considering I wasn't at all the baby. I was the sixth-oldest and eighth-youngest of all Nana's grandchildren, landing me somewhere near mid-eldest. I was the first child of her youngest child, which possibly could have meant something to her. I accepted my nana's words the way I've always accepted compliments that I felt I didn't deserve: I smiled politely and told myself not to take it to heart. Maybe she said this to all my cousins. Maybe there was some alternative definition of the word *favorite* that I didn't know about. Maybe I was the opposite of special and this was her way of making sure I didn't find out.

I was often singled out by my teachers as an example for my classmates, which always seemed wholly unjustified. I was smart but never the smartest in my class, kind but never went out of my way to help anyone, creative but unmotivated, neither popular nor unpopular, attentive but nonparticipatory, and between one and fifteen minutes late to school almost every single day of my entire life. But almost without fail, I was the teacher's pet. The one who never got in trouble even when I deserved it. The one who got second and third chances in the spelling bee because my teachers were more willing to believe that they'd heard me wrong than that I didn't know how to spell a word. I always felt that I had managed to trick adults without intending to, and was fearful that I would somehow reveal my true self to them.

Every compliment felt like a lie or a misunderstanding. When someone suggested I was cool, I couldn't help thinking, *What the fuck is your problem?*

But it started working the opposite way too. There was part of me that believed that I was the one who was wrong about me, that I just couldn't see my own greatness from my vantage point inside myself. When I was depressed, or felt like a complete piece of shit, or doubted my ability to do anything, there has always been a small but persistent voice saying, *You're actually kind of great.* My self-doubt and confidence became inextricably linked, like a tessellation. One side couldn't exist without the other.

"You have so much artistic talent," my nana told me when I was fifteen, after she heard I was showing an interest in art.

Oh yeah? I thought grouchily. *Name one medium I've worked in.* I believed she had no idea what my work looked like or what "artistic talent" meant or what she was talking about. I was somehow mad at her for not believing in me in the right way.

"Thank you," I said. I realized I believed in myself. Not because she said it, and not because anybody else (falsely, in my opinion) believed it of me. Despite all the concrete evidence I had to the contrary, and despite how embarrassing it was to admit, I believed in myself.

It has been with this embarrassing and self-inflicted confidence that I have written this book about myself, hoping to expose myself as the piece of shit I am, but also show how sweet and beautiful shit can be.

1

CHILD'S PLAY

I had my first sexual experience while watching *Child's Play* when I was six. I felt a mysterious but not unpleasant tingliness in the area that I referred to at the time as my "peepee." I had never felt such a sensation before. I think it may have had more to do with my position on the couch than with the content of the film, but because it was my first time experiencing the sensation, I attributed it to Chucky, the evil sentient doll.

I knew that this area of my body was somehow dangerous, because it was the part that was covered when I wore my bathing suit, and I had been told many times that the part of one's body that was covered by a bathing suit was off limits to anyone but myself and potentially the doctor.

"Chucky is cool," I said to my cousin Jenna, who was next to me on the couch. "Do you think Chucky is cool?"

"It's okay," Jenna said.

I adjusted my body so that a couch cushion rested against my peepee, and when Chucky was over I called my nana over and asked her to rewind the tape for me so I could watch it again.

"I think Chucky is really cool," I said.

After a little while, I went to the bathroom to investigate the tingling area. Then I felt the urge to pee, so I sat on the toilet and watched my peepee, trying to figure out where the pee was coming from.

"What is pee?" I asked my mom later that day, after my bath, as she powdered me with baby powder in front of the fireplace. My aunt Lynn was watching Fox News on TV next to us.

"It's just waste that your body doesn't need," my mom said.

"Where does it come out of?"

"Your pee hole."

"Your urethra," Aunt Lynn corrected.

"It's not my poop hole," I said. "I watched."

"No, it's a different one," my mom said. "You have two."

"You have three, if you really want to know," Lynn said, laughing.

"You're silly, Lynn," I said.

Jenna and I began asking our nana to rent us horror movies whenever we spent the night at her house, which was all the time. *Candyman. Pet Sematary. The People Under the Stairs. The Exorcist.* We watched them at night in the playroom, peeking through the blankets we wrapped ourselves in.

None of them had quite the same effect on me that Chucky had, but they still had an effect on me. My heart pounded for the endangered protagonists. The muscles in my abdomen tightened with anticipation as I began to understand the cues of the musical scores.

I made myself watch the gory, blood-soaked scenes. I was amazed that images of violence and terror were so accessible to me, so plainly displayed. Watching the scary parts all the way through was actually less scary than covering my eyes and imagining what was happening by the sound effects alone. But as scary as the films were, watching them gave me some sense of satisfaction. I was confronting my fear. If this was what being a grown-up was about, then maybe I could handle it.

•

A few months later, I had sex with my cousin Danny. At least that's what his sister, Jenna, told us we were doing, after she instructed us to crawl into bed and lie on top of each other fully clothed. The weight of Danny's body pressed against mine, first face to face and then spooning, as Jenna deemed appropriate. She was only a year older than Danny and me, but she had the weary experience of an old hooker.

"Stop picking your nose, Danny. You need to pay attention."

Earlier, Jenna had been mad at us because Danny and I wanted to play Teenage Mutant Ninja Turtles instead of Play-Doh. Then she'd said she knew of a game we could all play together. She had seen her parents doing it and she would tell us how it was done.

"I have to pee," Danny said.

"That's good. That's what you're supposed to do," Jenna said.

"Ew! Don't pee on me," I said. "I don't want to play anymore." I scrambled out from under Danny and jumped off the bed. I grabbed the Leonardo action figure to comfort me.

I felt deep shame and regret for what I had done. I didn't understand what sex was, but I was beginning to glean information about it from TV and from what Jenna told me. It was meant for grown-ups—I knew that much—and I was no grown-up. I also knew that sex was gross, even for grown-ups, because my nana would always say, "That's caca," any time there was nudity or kissing on television. The phrase "That's caca" had also been used when I ate a roly-poly in the backyard, and when my cousin Alana had picked up a piece of dry dog poop from the yard and threw it into the sun, smiling.

And I knew, from the way grown-ups dodged the "Where do babies come from?" question, that sex probably had something to do with that as well.

I didn't want anyone to ever find out about Danny and me, but

I also couldn't stop thinking about it. I felt overwhelmed trying to guess the consequences of what I had done.

"Let's tell Alana about sex," I said to Jenna. I figured if our three-year-old cousin started thinking and talking about sex, maybe I could feel less guilty about my own experience with it.

"Sex," we said to Alana, closing the door to the playroom. "Say 'sex.'"

"Set," said Alana. "Sets."

"Sex," Jenna said, repeatedly inserting her right index finger into the center of her left fist, our secret code for "sex."

"Sest," Alana said.

"You're stupid," Jenna said.

"Do you want another haircut?" I threatened. "Say it right."

We fashioned Alana's bangs into a jagged angled edge with some toenail clippers, then handed the toenail clippers to Alana and told her to go into the living room to show our moms her new look. When she wouldn't go, Jenna and I ran out of the room, yelling, "Help! Alana's cutting her hair!"

The next Christmas was The Best Christmas Ever. My family was on some social program that gave us day-old bakery goods and canned foods every week. But that year, we had gotten on a special program for Christmas. We got all the basic holiday foods, plus my gender and age were put on a list and an anonymous family bought gifts for me and my mom and her husband, Seth.

The anonymous family got me everything I could have ever thought to ask for: two Mattel-brand Barbies (so much better than the crappy hollow plastic dolls I sometimes got), Aesop's Fables cassette tapes, a bunch of awesome animal-shaped fabric coin purses, a neon winter jacket, a scarf and gloves, and a bright-pink plastic sled. From my mom I got an illustrated copy of *The Secret Garden* and a new bike helmet; from my nana and papa I got a used book about cats, a cat calendar, and two glass cat figurines; and from Santa I got five VHS tapes with home-recorded animated movies complete with commercials, just like the ones my nana sent me on a regular basis, and were even labeled in my nana's handwriting. Which is all to say that I was a little suspicious about Santa. My gut told me that the grown-ups were exaggerating his generosity and/or his ability to coordinate the entire holiday by himself. Maybe he had to work with the grown-ups to get gifts. Maybe I had been a little too eager receiving my nana's homemade VHS tapes, and they had taken my enthusiasm to mean that I loved homemade VHS tapes over all other toys. Maybe my nana had intercepted Santa, said something like, "I got this one. Take care of the other children."

My friend Tanja had gotten Barbies for Christmas too. She lived in the same apartment complex as my family, so we were allowed to hang out much later than we were with our other friends.

Her family was very modern. Tanja introduced me to snack foods I had never heard of, like Corn Nuts and NutRageous, and her mother allowed us to bathe together, something I had never done with a friend before. After the bath, Tanja and I were also allowed to play with our toys until my mom came to get me.

I was always a little hesitant, with new friends, to make my Barbies have sex. I would dance around the subject, make them hold hands and kiss, but Tanja's Barbies always started having sex in the first two minutes of play.

"They're having sex now," Tanja said, laying the Ken on top of the Barbie.

"Are they going to have a baby?" I said. "Having babies" seemed like the sexiest thing in the world to me.

"No," she said. "It's casual sex."

Sometimes the word still brought a sudden unshakable sense of doom. My whole body blushed with shame.

I had sex with my cousin, I thought. I closed my eyes and covered them with my hands for a few seconds to make the thoughts go away.

•

My mom and I visited Jenna and Danny's family after Christmas. They had moved to Oregon and I hadn't seen them in several months, and I was thrilled to be able to play with them again. They had had a depressing Christmas, my mom told me, so I wasn't supposed to talk to them about the gifts I'd gotten from the anonymous family.

My cousins and I went outside to throw a Frisbee and play with the dog while the grown-ups made dinner.

"Remember when we *did it*?" Danny asked me when Jenna had run away from us to fetch the Frisbee.

"No," I told him. "We didn't *do it*. Never talk about that. Never say that to me again."

"Okay, but you do remember, right?"

"No. I'm not talking about it."

Danny mentioning it made me feel much worse. It was confirmation that it had actually happened, and wasn't merely a realistic dream that I couldn't shake. I didn't yet know the words *pervert* or *deviant*, but I felt them innately. I was caca. I was gross and bad and everyone would know that, if I didn't hold on to this horrible secret forever.

It would be easy, I told myself. It had been so easy to pretend all day that I hadn't gotten such wonderful gifts from that anonymous family. It was easy to pretend that nothing had happened, that I was neither lucky nor gross.

But the more I tried not to think about it, the more I thought about it. I worried Danny would tell someone, that my mom would find out, or that maybe she already knew. Maybe she already knew I was caca and didn't love me as much as she used to. Maybe she thought less of me for not having the bravery to tell her.

"I had sex with Danny," I said to my mom a few days later. It came out suddenly, surprising me. It had been on my mind constantly, a dull, unrelenting nausea, and I couldn't bear the thought of feeling that way for the rest of my life.

I described what I had done, what Jenna had told us to do, how she had stood by the door to make sure her parents didn't come check on us, and that I didn't think I could ever forgive myself. I wished I would cry, to emphasize the point that I hated what I had done, that I felt bad about it all the time. But no tears would come.

"It's okay," my mom said, trying not to laugh. "That's not sex."

I considered initiating a hug but changed my mind.

"Next time just say you don't want to do that."

2

THE MEANING OF LIFE

I was lying under the swings in my backyard, throwing a swing up into the air and letting it fall toward my face before it sprang back up by the power of some mysterious gravitational force. I was trying to desensitize myself to the surprises of the world, equipping myself to resist what I felt was an embarrassing instinct to react to my environment and other people without logically deciding how to react.

I was also trying to summon a UFO. I was thinking very purposefully and singularly about it. I closed my eyes and reopened them dramatically, fully expecting to see a UFO, or two, or even a cluster of them, hovering above my house.

I wanted badly to believe in aliens. At eleven, I was already deeply atheist, and the lack of meaning in the world terrified me. I had a recurring unwanted thought, usually in bed at night, about what it would be like to die. I envisioned the darkest deep black space imaginable, large enough to encompass everything I knew and didn't know, everything I ever thought or had or loved rendered meaningless in a single moment, my consciousness ceasing completely. The thought made my chest hot, like the beginning of a panic attack, and I calmed myself by petting my arms and humming little songs.

The possibility of the existence of aliens gave me hope. If they existed, it would prove that humans could be completely ignorant about certain things. Important things. It would call into question everything we collectively believed in. We would have to throw everything out and start over. Maybe my unwanted thoughts about death could be eased by the fact that nobody could ever know anything for sure.

I also thought that if aliens did visit, because of my evident specialness and my blind resolve to believe in their existence, I would most likely be chosen to communicate their wishes to my fellow Earthlings. I would be pertinent to the needs of this alien culture, a culture I could not fathom but that would nevertheless also prove beneficial to me somehow. This would give me special privileges within their culture, the nature of which I could not begin to guess but that, if you twisted my arm, probably included access to secret knowledge about Earth, other planets, and the meaning of life, as well as the ability to teleport.

I did not, however, want to be taken into space. I was afraid of heights, for one thing. I was also somewhat disturbed by the idea of being in a foreign country, even if I was only floating above it. I would agree to be taken onto their spaceship and flown around North America and possibly certain parts of the ocean, as long as I could be home at a reasonable hour. I didn't want to find out what my nightly death thoughts felt like in space, unless those fears disappeared the moment I saw an alien, dispelling the lonely emptiness I experienced whenever I thought about outer space.

After a while I gave up trying to summon aliens, but I continued my practice of lying under the swing set and throwing the swing up to let it drop back down, preparing for future surprises that I could pretend to not be surprised by.

I started planning outdoor sleepovers in a tent in the backyard, hoping the extra time outdoors at night would increase my chances of seeing

UFOs. My friends and I would run around the yard until 1 a.m., playing hide-and-seek, trying to scare one another, and endlessly squealing. When we got tired, we would lie on the lawn looking up into the sky.

"Do you believe in aliens?" I said to my friend Lauren.

"Maybe," Lauren said. "That would be cool."

"Yeah," I said.

Late one night, as my friends and I settled into our tent to go to sleep, we saw beams from flashlights coming from the front of the house. When we saw the lights in the side yard coming toward us in the backyard, we jumped out of the tent and made a rush for the back door of my house. We watched from the kitchen window as three dark figures opened our tent and tore all the blankets out of it and onto the lawn. I assumed these figures were our angry neighbors, sick of me and my loud friends. I hoped we weren't going to get in trouble.

My mom's husband, Seth, had woken up from the noise of us running inside and slamming the door. We told him there were people in our tent and Seth went outside with a flashlight and yelled, "Hey!"

The figures quickly left through the side yard.

We ran to the other side of the house and looked out the living room window. I saw the three figures leave our driveway and heard them enter and pull away in a car that was obscured by the hedges in front of our yard. Then I saw a fourth figure running from the alleyway on the other side of the house. He ran down the street in the opposite direction of the other figures, got into a truck, and drove away.

"It was probably security guards," my mom said over and over, as if trying to convince herself that the intruders weren't dangerous. We lived in a gated community called Hidden Valley, and sometimes, because of my lack of respect for the curfew or other people's property, we'd had to deal with the community's hired guards.

"Why would they go through the tent instead of knocking on the door?" I said.

"They're assholes, I guess," she said. "I should call the police on their asses."

•

Jenna came down from Oregon for summer vacation that year, and we spent every moment together, alternating between staying at my house and our nana and papa's. One evening my cousin Amy slept over too. We turned the lights off in my room and tried to conjure spirits using scented candles and a handmade Ouija board. As I didn't believe in spirits, I secretly tried to conjure aliens. There was no reason the aliens wouldn't choose to communicate through this medium. I moved the planchette across the board, stopping at the letters that "felt right" to me. I didn't tell the others what I was doing, but I also didn't consider it cheating. I thought if aliens did exist and they were trying to communicate with us, it was just as likely that they would choose to control the planchette as it was that they would choose to control my subconscious mind. I was allowing them to choose this path, if that was easier for them.

Often, instead of meaningful words or sentences, I would spell out lines of pure gibberish. This didn't discourage me, though. I took it as a sign that whatever the aliens were trying to spell was too esoteric for my understanding, or that my subconscious mind was too powerful to be controlled by aliens.

In the middle of a series of far too many consonants, Amy started screaming and ran out of my room. I followed her, laughing, thinking she was pretending to have seen a ghost. Jenna came out of my room moments later.

"I saw a man looking in your window," Amy said. "I'm not playing. Someone was outside." I had a large window in my room that had no blinds or curtains. It faced a narrow alleyway filled with bushes.

"I saw it, too," Jenna said. She seemed shaken. "I'm not going back in there. Where's your mom?"

"What did it look like?" I said, hoping to hear a description of a gray alien.

"I don't know," Amy said. "I just saw a face and ran."

We knocked on my mom's door and I told her what Amy and Jenna had seen.

"Go around front and see if anyone is in the alleyway," my mom said. "I'll go out back and see if anyone is in the yard."

Amy was too scared to leave the house, so Jenna and I went out front. We didn't see anything, so we went back inside and then to the backyard. My mom was standing next to our porch, swinging a baseball bat at the air in front of her.

"What are you doing?" I said.

"Ahhh," my mom yelled, and continued swinging the bat.

Jenna ran back into the house and began screaming while running circles around the kitchen and living room. I followed her.

"What are you doing?" I said again. She continued to scream and run circles. I went back outside and my mom was beating the ground with the baseball bat. I went back inside and Jenna was still running in circles. Feeling helpless and confused, I sat down on the couch with Amy.

Eventually my mom came in from the backyard and locked the door.

"I saw glowing red eyes," she said. "Like a dog's eyes. But it didn't come after me. It stayed where it was, as if it were on a leash."

After that night I started hearing a weird sound outside my window at night. It was a distinct scraping sound that occurred inconsistently throughout the week. I might hear it on Wednesday at 10 p.m., and then not again until the weekend.

I thought I heard the same sound coming from the kitchen during the daytime once, but then it was identified as my mom rubbing a kitchen knife against a knife sharpener stick.

"A deranged murderer," I said flatly to Jenna when she heard the sound too.

"Don't say that!" she said.

•

I was given rollerblades for my birthday. I would rollerblade in circles around our block. The lot behind our house was empty, and I liked to look into our backyard from the front of the lot. I would try to see the house as someone unfamiliar with it would see it. Did we look All-American, with our swing set and tiny, half-assed garden? Did we look trashy, with the plastic orange safety mesh stapled around our porch railing in lieu of wooden posts? Sometimes my mom would be outside on the lawn with my baby brother, River, and I would wave to them as I skated by.

One day as I skated by, I noticed a car parked in front of the empty lot. Inside, two people who resembled the parents from *Matilda* were pointing and gesturing at the back of my house. I skated back around to the front of my house, where my mom was watching River scoot around in his play car.

"Mom," I said. "Some weird people are looking at the back of our house from Bear Valley Road."

"Who are they?"

"I don't know!"

I skated around the loop again and they were still stalled in front of the empty lot. I slowed down to try to hear what they were saying. They watched me as I skated by, and then sped off.

"This weird car slowed down in front of our house," my mom said when I had gotten back around the block.

"Was it a white car?"

"Yeah," she said.

"That's them. So trippy," I said.

"If they come around again I'm going to chase them down the street," Seth said when my mom told him what happened. "This is private property. You can't just spy on people."

I had initially hoped that the *Matilda* couple were aliens disguised as people, like in the movie *Men in Black*, but now I was worried that they might be CIA agents, targeting my house because they knew I was trying to communicate with aliens.

But maybe that meant I was closer to reaching them than I thought.

My friends Lauren and Lauren and I had a sleepover in a tent on one of the Laurens' back porch. In the morning, Lauren's mom was going to drive us to the mall in Santa Rosa to buy school clothes. I hadn't really wanted to go shopping because my mom wasn't going to give me any money, and it seemed boring to watch my friends pick out clothes when I couldn't. But I'd agreed to go because I wanted to be part of the tent sleepover.

We lit candles in the tent and made up ghost and alien stories until we fell asleep. I woke up in the middle of the night with an intense pain on my left arm. I couldn't see what was happening to it in the dark, but I could feel that something was on my arm, and I rubbed off whatever it was as I unzipped the tent and went inside to find the kitchen light. Lauren's mom heard me and came out from her bedroom. She inspected my arm with me. What looked like white, bloated skin was falling off my arm where I had been rubbing it.

"Is that wax?" she said.

"Maybe," I said. We woke up Lauren and Lauren and inspected the tent. The candles had been put out and were intact where we had left them.

"Maybe the flashlight battery leaked on your arm," Lauren's mom said.

"Maybe," I said, suspecting the real explanation was far more *out of this world*. Perhaps aliens were trying to mark me, indicate that I was a human to be trusted, helped out, or lifted into the air for an amusing trip around familiar North American skies.

We inspected the flashlights. Their batteries and cases looked the same as always, and they appeared to be functioning normally.

"What the hell," Lauren's mom said.

In the morning, I went home to tend to my injury instead of going shopping in Santa Rosa. I pretended to be disappointed.

The scraping sound continued outside my bedroom window that night. I hadn't heard it in a few days, and I had missed it. The slow, rhythmic scraping had begun to have a calming effect on me.

I didn't really believe there was an alien outside my window, but the sound felt connected to the aliens. It seemed as if all the inexplicable events of the summer were connected somehow, even though none of them made sense on their own and didn't seem to fit together either.

As obsessed with aliens as I thought I was, I can't remember doing any actual research or looking into other people's alien sightings or consuming alien culture. Alien movies scared me, and the creepy, violent nature of movie aliens didn't fit my idea of what aliens were. Stories of UFO sightings and abductions by dopey Middle Americans didn't paint the picture I had in my head either. Government alien cover-ups were okay, but focused too much on the government, and not enough on the personalities of aliens. Crop circles were interesting to me, and fit in with my idea of what aliens were (mysterious but screwball). I liked watching TV shows about crop circles, though I never sought them out.

I was mostly interested in my own fabricated idea of aliens. The aliens I thought about were gentle, loving, and highly invested in my well-being but not necessarily in the well-being of anyone else. They were surrogate parents who would someday lift me from my Earthly troubles and explain away all the things that scared me.

One night after having dinner at McDonald's, we came home to find the front door of our house unlocked and ajar. We looked around our house suspiciously, tiptoeing around corners and swinging open closet doors.

Later in the night, Seth complained of a clicking sound in the earpiece of the phone.

"I think we've been bugged," he said. "And the front door . . ."

"I don't think we've been bugged and I think the door thing is unrelated," my mom said, sounding irritated. "One of us probably forgot to shut the door all the way and the wind pushed it open."

Seth called the community security guards anyway, and reported a break-in.

"We'll write it down, but we don't really investigate that kind of thing," the security guard said. "What street do you live on again?"

The security guard told Seth they had just caught a Peeping Tom a block from our house, looking into a window at a teenage girl. The Peeping Tom was a landscaper hired by the community board to perform routine maintenance, but had been fired before the incident.

"Jesus Christ," my mom said. "Why the hell do we live here again?"

I got a chill remembering the face Amy saw in my window. We were being watched that night, and maybe many nights before and after that night. Maybe it also explained the strange scraping sound.

I felt scared and violated, but since he was caught before we found out about him, I didn't feel worried about my safety. I mostly felt disappointed. A Peeping Tom was not paranormal at all. In fact, it underlined my need for an extraterrestrial intervention. *This planet sucks*, I thought.

That night, as I lay on the lawn counting shooting stars, I heard the familiar scraping sound coming from the alley by my bedroom window.

Aha, I thought, using a British accent in my head for some reason. *Perhaps there is mystery yet on this Earth.*

3

VANDAL

The first house we ever toilet-papered belonged to somebody we didn't know at all. My friends and I had chosen the house for being a safe-but-not-too-far distance from my house, very distant from the Hidden Valley security guard shacks, somewhat secluded from other houses, but close to a variety of trees and shrubs and fences—places we could hide if we needed to.

We did a terrible job that first time—a few throws over a tree and the rest wadded up and tossed around the lawn before we ran away giggling—but the experience filled me with adrenaline.

My house had become a popular house for sleepovers, because my mom would let us "sneak" out as much as we wanted. With my core group of friends—Catlin, Anabelle, Lauren, and Lauren—I would walk around the empty golf courses that were off-limits during the day. We would lie on the impossibly fine-cut grass and talk about secret stuff, because that time of night in an off-limits place was made for secrets.

It was my mom who had first mentioned toilet-papering.

"You guys have never toilet-papered a house?" she had said. "Ever? How weird."

That first night, my friends and I left through the sliding glass door in my bedroom, my mom whispering behind us, "Don't get caught! I'll leave a light on for you guys."

After that, I became obsessed with toilet-papering houses. Strangers' houses, houses of people I vaguely knew, houses I wished I lived in, houses I used to live in that were now occupied by other tenants, the house of the teacher I had never had class with but who I heard was mean, the house of the people who'd refused to buy Save the Rainforest T-shirts from me the year before when I was trying to win a *Cat in the Hat* hat by outselling my classmates.

Everything about toilet-papering houses was gratifying: the supply organization, the sneaking around, the security guards driving around looking for vandals like us, the potential for punishment. But possibly the best part was riding my bike past the house the next morning to check whether it was cleaned up or not. Knowing that the evidence of my vandalism was available for all to see in the light of day made me feel powerful. I liked thinking about the confusion I'd inspired in residents the next morning, and how I'd never be suspected because I was just a little girl.

That year we were twelve, and friend dynamics were beginning to feel more complicated. There was always some issue between us. Catlin would be mad at one of the Laurens, or Anabelle and Lauren would be fighting, or Catlin and I would be competing for one of the Laurens' attention, or Anabelle would be convincing us that Catlin wasn't our friend. The five of us rarely hung out all together. This was fine with me, as it was easier to sneak around with only two or three people. It also allowed me to rotate who I would take with me toilet-papering so that I could satisfy my insatiable enthusiasm for it without anybody getting burned out.

But eventually my core group of friends became bored with it and I had to recruit different friends, and when the new recruits became bored with it, I asked my cousins to sleep over and made them go out with me, and when they got bored as well, I asked people from school who I didn't consider friends but who were willing to hang out with me, and when they became bored with it I finally gave it up, unwilling to go by myself.

My friends still liked sleeping over and sneaking out, but only to meet up with boys. I was fine with this in theory. We didn't hang out much with boys at school, and it seemed exciting to hang out with people outside of a classroom setting. But usually we would spend the whole night calling different boys, trying to find someone who would be willing and able to meet up with us, wasting it on unsuccessful coordination. It was time that would have been better spent, in my opinion, toilet-papering houses.

Sometimes, though, we were able to arrange for boys to meet up with us. We had a few spots around the neighborhood that were safe from parents and security guards: a mysterious half-buried empty pipe large enough for ten of us to crawl into, a house that was being renovated that was often left unlocked, and Lauren's stepbrother's bedroom, which was a separate granny unit next to the main house.

We would play Truth or Dare and take turns kissing each other and, if it was my turn to determine what the dare would be, spitting into each other's mouths a certain number of times. Eventually all my friends would disappear with a boy to participate in non-dare-based kissing, and I would be left with someone like Lucas, who had a lazy eye and who I was strongly attracted to despite my own desire not to be.

I was never sure if I was attracted to him because of or despite his lazy eye. He was cool and confident but still managed to be nice, which wasn't something the other cool, confident boys in my class seemed to be able to pull off. He didn't seem to be self-conscious or apologetic about his lazy eye, which I found intimidating and inspiring, but also unrelatable.

Because of my confused feelings, I tried hard not to develop a crush on him, and my efforts were mostly successful.

"What street do you live on?" I would say, trying to sound courteous, which I felt was the opposite of flirtatious.

"Powder Horn Road," Lucas would say, simultaneously looking at me and through my neighbor's open window.

"Oh, that's a really nice part of town. What do your parents do for a living?"

Sometimes after Truth or Dare, I would be left alone with Duncan.

Duncan sat in front of me in both morning English class and afternoon Science class. Every day in English after we were given our assignment, he would ask me for a few sheets of lined paper. I would roll my eyes, rip them out of my binder in dramatic faux indignation, and tell him that he owed me quite a lot of lined paper and that I was considering charging him interest for my lost resources. In Science, if I was wearing my giant furry platform shoes, he would turn around in his chair and pet them and tell me he liked them and I would tell him they were my least favorite shoes and I was just trying to wear them out so I wouldn't have to wear them anymore. If I didn't wear them he would ask me why I wasn't wearing them.

Duncan was my age, but he looked a lot younger, like a weirdly tall five-year-old. He had a bowl cut, a slight stutter, and was bow-legged, and I was fully in love with him.

One night, someone we knew had been given access to some house near where we were. It was a friend of Lauren's older brother whose parents were out of town. We went to the house and someone turned on some soft-core porn that was in the VHS player. We shared three cans of beer between the six of us. Lauren sat to next to Nick who sat next to Brad who sat next to Catlin. I sat to the right of Catlin and Duncan sat next to me, at the end of the couch. The sound wasn't working, so there was no narrative for the couple on screen as they took each other's clothes off on an overcast beach, and no character motivation when the man began to caress the woman's breasts and stomach. I felt annoyed that the TV was on and that we were all just sitting in silence, wasting the time we had together.

When the movie ended, our friends broke up into twos to go

make out, and Duncan and I walked around outside until we found some quiet cul-de-sac where we sat down and talked about my giant furry platforms, which I stupidly wasn't wearing; English class; homework; the quality of the cafeteria food; and a cold that Duncan may or may not have been coming down with, he wasn't sure.

Talking alone with Duncan was as good as or better than kissing him would have been. It felt so intimate, and I was eager to see what would happen when I saw him in class on Monday.

"Duncan wanted to kiss you," Catlin told me the next day. "He told his friends he wanted to but he didn't want to give you his cold."

"Aww," I said.

It was endearing to me that he wanted to kiss me but hadn't. It pointed to a possible shared fear of intimacy and/or sexual exploration probably caused by a sensitivity to people that made us thoughtful and emotional, which had the potential to mean that we were alike in ways our friends couldn't understand, which could someday bring us together in a more meaningful and beautiful way than what our friends were able to experience with each other by kissing so quickly.

"You had him all to yourself during the porno," Catlin said later. "You could have done anything."

"Porno? What porno? Oh, that weird silent film that lacked even the most basic plot structure? Oh, Duncan was sitting next to me during that? Oh, I hadn't noticed." I felt a pang of semi-horny regret for the missed opportunity. But there was nothing I would have done differently, I reasoned. It had been the perfect night.

When Anabelle and I hung out without our other friends, she liked to sneak out and meet up with older boys. And by "older boys," I guess I mean "men." More specifically, tattooed men with facial scars who hadn't lived with their parents for years and who offered us beer and weed when we knocked on their door at 9:30 p.m. Maybe I sensed trouble, or maybe I just wasn't as bad or as cool as Anabelle was, but I would beg her to go back home with me when it was still early, only a couple hours after Community Youth Curfew, well before I ever wanted to go home when we were vandalizing property or hanging out with boys our own age.

I wanted to be outside, shrouded by the anonymity of the night, causing mischief I wouldn't be held responsible for, inspiring feelings I couldn't really understand in people I would never know. I did not want to be sitting politely in some stranger's apartment, hoping he didn't want to molest us.

"I want to be outside," I whispered. "Let's run around on the golf course and let the security guards chase us around."

"I don't want to," Anabelle said, loudly enough for everyone in the room to hear. "I'm having fun here."

"Let's move the flags away from the holes," I whispered. "That sounds so fun."

"I don't feel like it," she said. She walked away from me and started hugging a shirtless man with an enormous back tattoo that read MAXINE. I sat back down on a couch, inhaling secondhand pot smoke, and wondered why I wasn't attracted to these adult men that Anabelle found so appealing. They were creepy and seemed filthy and talked about stupid things. I found their shirtless torsos repulsive and their high-pitched stony laughter menacing.

It occurred to me that it was possible I was a lesbian, even though I wasn't attracted to women. Maybe I just hadn't noticed being attracted to women. But I wasn't attracted to men, either. Sometimes I was attracted to boys my age, sometimes to older thirteen-year-olds (and sometimes, shamefully, to eleven-year-olds). But my crushes were so childlike and innocent compared to Anabelle's obvious horniness for a man who seemed so capable of actual sexuality.

There were other indicators too, such as the prevalence of overalls and striped T-shirts in my wardrobe, or the fact that I liked *South Park* and Comedy Central's *Premium Blend*, which I now recognized were shows that none of my girl friends ever watched.

I was temporarily comforted by the fact that I had felt compelled to tape posters of male celebrities all over my bedroom walls—Jonathan Taylor Thomas, Leonardo DiCaprio, Kurt Cobain, Joseph Gordon-Levitt, and Hanson—but I soon realized that this group of men conspicuously favored long luxurious hair, which I thought could be an indicator of some hidden homosexual desire.

I had heard about gay people marrying members of the opposite sex before realizing they were gay. I told myself that it was a good thing I was figuring it out before I had wasted most of my life mistakenly thinking I was straight. Maybe I could start embracing my lesbianism now, and by the time I was an adult it would be no big deal. Maybe I was lucky.

Then again, I really did feel attracted to Duncan, and thought about him a lot in a way that seemed romantic. I imagined running my fingers along the edge of his bowl cut. I wore my giant furry platforms just to get his attention. When I found a note from him to one of his friends on the ground at school, I took it home and analyzed the handwriting using handwriting analysis websites, and then folded the note and put it in the small jewelry box where I kept things I wanted to cherish. I had definitely never felt that way about any girl.

Still, I hadn't even thought to kiss Duncan when we had been alone. Did that indicate that I wasn't interested in kissing or being sexual? Perhaps I just wasn't a sexual person. Or perhaps my lack of initiative was more indicative of my fear of rejection. If so, did that fear necessarily mean I was heterosexual? Maybe I was confused. Maybe being a lesbian would somehow postpone my need to address my sexuality. Maybe I was attracted to boys my age because they sort of looked like adult lesbians.

It would be just my luck to have to be a lesbian, I thought, annoyed but resigned, in the same tone someone else might think, *Ugh, I'm going to have to write my report tonight*. I decided that if I did turn out to be a lesbian, I would simply refuse to be attracted to women, realizing as I was having the thought that it didn't make any sense.

I heard the shirtless tattooed man tell Anabelle that he wanted to show her his collection of *Playboy*s that he kept in his bedroom and I leaped up, yelling that we needed to go. I didn't want Anabelle to look at a man's *Playboys*. I didn't want her to be a sexual person, because that might mean that I was becoming a sexual person, and I did not yet want to face that.

"WE NEED TO GO! We need to go right now," I said, pulling Anabelle by her arm, inexplicably giggling. I was being an insane spaz and I did not care. "We have to go! Right now is when we have to go, and I'm going, and you're going, too!" I said.

Anabelle knew it and the creepy tattooed man knew it and I knew it: I wasn't cool. I was an embarrassing loser, a pathetic virgin, and probably a lesbian.

We didn't see any security guards out, but I ran home through the golf course as quickly as I could anyway. Anabelle yelled after me to slow down the entire way, but I ignored her.

After that night, I made deals with my friends if they wanted to sleep over: "If you want to visit a boy, we have to toilet-paper a house first. Otherwise, you can sneak out of your own house." It was great leverage, because my friends had attentive and protective parents who made it much harder to sneak out of their own houses. Plus my house was in a better location, central in terms of many of the favored boys.

The last house I ever toilet-papered belonged to the family of a boy named Mark, who had my bus route and who I found annoying. He was loud and secure despite being painfully uncool. His family lived a couple of blocks from mine and they had a dog statue at the end of their driveway. I don't know why, but the dog statue pissed me off. *What the hell would you need a dog statue for?* I thought. *Just get a real dog, losers.* Because I hadn't been out toilet-papering for a couple months, I had a lot of pent-up vandalism energy. This time, I wanted to do more than just throw toilet paper around. Anabelle and I filled two two-liter soda bottles with condiments, garbage, and left-over spaghetti, added a little bit of water, and shook them to create a chunky, liquidy jelly. We took these bottles, along with some eggs and toilet paper, to Mark's house in the middle of the night. Not only did we empty the bottles of sludge onto the front door, steps, and exterior walls of the house, and throw eggs onto their garage door and car, and cover their trees with toilet paper, but we also picked up and carried their bird bath from the yard and placed it on the driveway, dragged their dog statue into the middle of their lawn, and moved other various lawn ornaments and flower pots into what I believed was an aesthetically awkward and embarrassing display. The whole operation took well over an hour. When I was satisfied with our work, we went to the house next door, to an open garage where some tattooed men Anabelle knew were drinking and hanging out. I was so pleased with myself that I even took a few sips of beer while Anabelle recounted our shenanigans to the guys. We stayed over very late, and when I started falling asleep on the outdoor couch, one of the tattooed men suggested that Anabelle and I go home.

Before we woke up the next morning, Anabelle's mom called my house demanding to know where we had been the night before. My mom swore we had been at home all night, but her lies did nothing for our case. We were caught. The security guards had talked to Mark's neighbors to see if they knew anything about the vandalism, and they had given them Anabelle's first and last name, and the security guards had called Anabelle's mom looking for us.

"Shit," Anabelle said. "Fuck. Shit. Fuck." Anabelle's mom was very strict. She had once been grounded for three weeks for taking her hair out of a ponytail at school, and I'm pretty sure I'm not leaving any details out of that story or exaggerating it. Anabelle and I both knew that she was a goner. We said goodbye as though she were dying.

I thought about Mark, wondering what he thought about what Anabelle and I had done to his house, or if he had any idea that it had something to do with him.

I tried to imagine what it must feel like to be a twelve-year-old boy who is the random target of two twelve-year-old girls. I wondered if he would tell his friends or if it would be a shameful secret that destroyed his confidence and instilled in him a fear and distrust of women that would last into his adulthood, eventually costing him thousands of dollars in therapy and prescription medication or, worse, leading him to an out-of-control pill addiction, a life of crime, and ruined relationships with everyone and everything he ever grew to care about.

I didn't hate Mark before we toilet-papered his house, but I hated him now, because this bleak image of his future made me feel guilty, and that is how I have always chosen to deal with guilt.

Anabelle and I were each given forty hours of community service, but I never worked a minute of my share of them, because my mom didn't make me.

4

PUNKS NOT DEAD

The road from our house to the hospital was called Butts Canyon, and to me it was the most beautiful road in the county. There were very few houses or businesses, only tall oaks and thick grass. I decided that I would live among the trees there if I ever found myself homeless. I would build a cabin from fallen branches with the outdoorsman skills I never showed any sign of possessing but I was sure I would immediately develop if they became necessary. I'd harvest berries and nuts, and make friends with the local animals who would teach me, through gentle nudges and subtle gestures, how to live off the land.

My mom and I drove through Butts Canyon two evenings a week to clean offices at the hospital. My stepdad, Seth, had suffered a minor tailbone injury that he'd thought he could exaggerate to qualify for Federal Disability Insurance, so he'd quit his job, drastically increased his weed intake, and began looking into disability claim requirements. To me it seemed like he wouldn't qualify for it, since he made a full recovery pretty quickly, but I didn't really know how that stuff worked. My mom took the office-cleaning job to make up for his lost income, and I went along to help, as well as to avoid any one-on-one time with Seth.

It took an hour to drive to the hospital, and on the way we listened to my mom's old cassette tapes: the Clash, Sex Pistols, the Cure, and the Smiths. She had found them in an old box. I could remember hearing some of the songs earlier in my childhood, but most I had not heard before, or didn't remember. My mom recounted old stories from when she had listened to this music, who her friends had been, what the songs had meant to her at the time, and what they meant to her now.

"*I wasn't born so much as I fell out, nobody seemed to notice me.*" My mom sang along to the gravelly voice on the Clash cassette. She had a way of singing in harmony with the music, but just a little ahead or a little behind the actual song. I believed she was a musical genius.

"That's how I always felt as kid," she said. "I always thought this song was about me."

"Were you lonely?" I said.

"I felt invisible. My brothers and sisters acted crazy and fought with each other for our parents' attention, and it wasn't worth it for me to even try. I was the youngest. I was left out of everything. One time I tried out for the basketball team, and my mom said she would pick me up after tryouts because I was going to miss the after-school bus. But she never came to pick me up. I just stood in front of the school until ten, when my sister Gina rode by on her motorcycle and picked me up. My mom and dad had been at the bar all day and forgot about me."

"How did Gina know to drive by the school?" I said.

"Our mom probably finally remembered that she was supposed to pick me up and told Gina to come get me."

"What does 'lost in the supermarket' mean?" I asked, referring to the chorus of the song.

"I think of it as the feeling of being somewhere very commonplace that you think should feel comfortable and easy, and feeling lost and scared there."

I was put in charge of vacuuming the offices while my mom

wiped surfaces and emptied garbage bins. There was rarely anything to suck up from the cheap, flat carpet, so it was mostly a matter of moving the vacuum around and snooping through desk drawers and cabinets until my mom was done. I considered stealing from the supply cabinets, as I had come to fetishize Post-it notes and binder clips and other office paraphernalia, but I didn't want my mom to get in trouble and lose the job.

When we were finished, my mom would let me buy pumpkin pie from the vending machine in the hospital lobby, and I would eat it as we drove back through Butts Canyon.

With so much time on his hands, Seth became obsessed with get-rich-quick schemes. He bought into a tea tree oil product line, which was like Avon for people who wanted tea tree oil in every cleaning and skin product they owned, as well as in toothpaste, dog food, and vitamins. The setup was that you had to sell a certain number of products each month to maintain seller status. But because he couldn't find any customers, Seth purchased the products himself, hoping to sell them later when he found clients. The shampoos and detergents piled up under the kitchen sink and in the bathroom and on the shelves in the garage, and ultimately my mom had to cancel her credit card to prevent the company from charging us for any more products.

The other get-rich-quick idea that Seth got caught up in was website banner ads. Banner ads were the long, skinny advertisements that you would see on the bottoms or tops of web pages, and they were pretty big in the nineties. Many companies offered to pay a fraction of a penny for each time someone clicked their banner ad on your website, or maybe a few pennies if a purchase was ultimately made. If you had a hugely successful website with lots of traffic, you could potentially make a few dollars here and there. The websites Seth made were 100 percent banner ads, rows and rows of banner ads to scroll through and nothing else.

"Why would anyone ever visit your website?" I asked Seth. "I'm not even trying to be mean. I'm just honestly wondering who in his right mind would ever visit a website as stupid and pointless as yours, let alone click on one of your stupid idiotic banner ads enough times to make it worth it for you to have set the stupid page up in the first place."

"Shut up, go away," Seth said. "I'll have you know I got twenty hits yesterday."

"Yeah, probably from you refreshing your browser twenty times," I said.

I knew a thing or two about the web. I had, for the last couple of years, been obsessively making websites about Hanson and Jamiroquai and New Radicals. I'd collect information and photos about the bands from other websites and put it all back together in what I thought was a more cohesive way. Then I'd add GIFs and maybe a poll about which Hanson brother you would most like to share a bagel with or what you thought Jamiroquai's "Cosmic Girl" was really about. Though I preferred web rings, which connected sites to other sites that had similar content, I had done a little research about the potential profitability of banner ads, and basically had found that they were mostly a pointless endeavor, especially for a small site that nobody went to, and *especially* for a site that had no content other than advertising.

Seth spent hours per day clicking on his own banner ads, and sometimes purchasing the items the banner ads were advertising. As far as I know, he never saw any payment for his efforts.

"You need *content*," I said. "Why don't you make a website about something that interests you? Or that might interest someone, any human being in the entire world. And then place banner ads that have something to do with the content of your website?"

"Like what?" he said.

"I don't know. How about a website about all the shitty song lyrics you write when you're stoned?"

My cousin Jenna and I had found pages and pages of his song lyrics with dozens of misspellings written in his childlike scrawl and stuffed into one of my Hello Kitty folders. The lyrics were shockingly horrible. Jenna and I memorized some of the particularly horrible lines, like *luckary lady, soft and shady* and *I wanna touch your caress* and *thinking of you thinking of me thinking of you thinking of me*, and sang them to each other randomly to make each other laugh.

"By the way, I could do spell-check on them, if you want," I said.

"You are a fucking asshole."

"No, I really liked 'Luckary Lady,'" I said, laughing, enunciating his misspelling. "I think it could be a hit."

Seth and my mom fought a lot. Yelling and stomping around, mostly, but sometimes the fights became physically aggressive, and they would throw things or grab each other or make physical threats. When this happened I would take River and my new baby sister, Kylie, into my bedroom and read books to them or dress them up in my clothes and take photographs. We would hear things crashing around, glass breaking, furniture moving, one of them yelling through a locked door. I'd turn up my stereo to drown out the noise, and the three of us would dance around in my room.

Other times when my mom and Seth fought, I called my nana from the phone in my bedroom and explained to her that if my mom was ever murdered I wanted to live with her, but that I couldn't live with her without River and Kylie, so could she ensure that we would all live with her and that River and Kylie wouldn't have to live with Seth? Even though Seth was their dad? Was that possible, legally? Could she promise me that we would run from the law if we needed to?

When the fighting went on for hours, Nana and Papa, and Aunt Lynn and Alana, who lived with them, would make the forty-five-minute drive over to our house to check on us and, if it was a weekend or vacation from school, pick the three of us up and take us back to their house.

"I'm sick of you calling your *nanny* all the time," Seth said, ripping my phone cord out of the wall after I told him and my mom that Nana was coming over to rescue us.

"Don't break her phone cord," my mom said in a weary voice. "You're both being unreasonable."

I was frustrated by her lack of emotion with regard to my phone, my only connection to the outside world when they were tearing the house apart. I was frustrated that she would equate my desire to ask for help when I felt scared and alone with someone breaking my only means to get that help. I was frustrated that she had never made more of an effort to get Seth and me to like each other and, when it became clear that we never would, that she decided it would be fine if her daughter spent her entire childhood living with someone who hated her. And I was frustrated that there wasn't even a good reason for any of this to happen, because their relationship was a complete failure, by her own admission.

I began blaming my mom for every fight I had with Seth, every fight they had with each other, every bad day made worse by his mocking my feelings, every moment my siblings were stuck in my bedroom listening to "MMMBop" at full volume when they didn't want to be, every *Teen Beat* magazine I had to live without because Seth was spending our family's money on pyramid schemes.

I pretty much knew that Seth wouldn't kill my mom, but I started wishing for there to be a close call, something that would prove to my mom how heartless and pathetic and mean he was, something that would force her to leave him for good. I hated him, and he hated me too. I knew this because we were pretty open about it.

"I hate you, Seth," I would say frequently.

"I hate you, too," he would say. "I really do."

"I wish you would die."

"I wish you would go live with your nana."

"I'd be much happier living with Nana, but I'd rather continue making you miserable."

"You're such a fucking punk."

"You're the punk," I said. "You have it written on your ugly arm."

Seth had a tattoo on his forearm of a rudimentary and weirdly one-dimensional snake/dragon, whose flat, colored body covered a semi-visible, older, possibly stick-and-poke tattoo that read PUNKS NOT DEAD in uppercase letters. The snake/dragon tattoo, which existed solely to cover up PUNKS NOT DEAD, had been a measure taken to present himself as an employable adult, as well as a somewhat embarrassing and un-punk admission that, despite his previously held opinion on the subject, punk was, in fact, really dead.

The phrase "punks not dead" seemed to imply an argument with an unheard voice that insisted punk *was* dead. A voice, I guessed, that originated inside Seth himself, a small but persistent part of him that was trying to make him feel bad about punk being dead, a voice that Seth tried to drown out with a shitty tattoo.

Now the snake tattoo that covered PUNKS NOT DEAD was an admission that even his own beliefs were not worth holding on to. It was a sign of his weakness and self-doubt that something he once thought important enough to permanently display on his body could be later renounced.

I signed up for an internet chat service called ICQ. I had used chat rooms before, but ICQ was superior in that it saved your contacts in a buddy list and you could therefore talk to the same people all the time. My cousin Jenna was on my buddy list, and we would chat occasionally, but mostly I talked to strangers.

"A/S/L?" I'd ask, and the stranger would give either a real or made-up age, sex, and location. Then I would give a real or made-up age, sex, and location. The conversation would be steered by this initiating information, though neither party would ever know if it was real or imaginary. In chat rooms, where anonymity was enforced by the sheer unlikelihood that you would ever talk to the same people ever again, I tended to be more creative in my A/S/L descriptions. But on ICQ I found that I was a lot more honest about my A/S/L.

"12/Female/California," I'd say. I found that most people would stay and chat regardless of what I said.

I talked to an Australian boy my age who asked for my mailing address and sent me photographs of himself playing "football," with notes on the back that seemed to be written by his mother: *Here is Johnny playing football with his classmate, Brent.*

I talked to an old woman about astrology.

I talked to a Spice Girl, whose identity had to be kept secret and who was only authorized to confirm that she was "one of the Spice Girls."

"Why did you marry Seth?" I asked my mom as we drove to the hospital one night.

"He was a lot different when we were younger," she said. "He was very gentle and shy and quiet."

"Sometimes I wish it was just me and you still," I said.

"Me too."

"I hate Seth, Mom," I said.

"I know, Chelsea," she said.

"He's really rude and mean. And Mom? You know he doesn't like me. Why do you want to be with someone who doesn't like me?"

"He had a really hard childhood. His stepdad beat him up all the time, and when he was little his mom became a Jehovah's Witness and they stopped celebrating his birthday or any other holiday. People at school always picked on him and beat him up because he was scrawny and weird. He's been through a lot."

"I don't care," I said.

I'd met Seth's mom once, years before. I tried to imagine her letting someone beat up her children. I tried to imagine how Seth felt then—not just the feeling of being beaten up, but the feeling of knowing that his mom was allowing that, or at least wasn't stopping it or leaving the man responsible for it. I tried to imagine what might have happened to her in her childhood that caused her to be so weak and indifferent. Seth's family tree splayed in my head, each parent worse than the one before, each the spawn of some greater evil, probably originating from some hellish demon. From this perspective, Seth didn't seem so horrible. He was not as horrible as his parents, who were not as horrible as their parents, which was something like progress.

I thought of a tiny, child-size Seth, anticipating a birthday party the year his mom decided to stop celebrating it, waiting for a gift or dessert that wouldn't come.

"They really didn't do anything for his birthday?" I said.

"I think his mom usually gave him a pomegranate," my mom said.

"Just a pomegranate?"

"Sad, huh?" she said, and turned up the music.

I wondered how I fit into the larger picture of Seth's life. Was I the next victim in the generations of neglect and abuse? Or was I inadvertently turning into yet another bully whose senseless torture Seth had to overcome?

It was difficult to remember where our hatred of each other had started. I was seven when he married my mom, too young to hate someone with no reason. I had been excited at their wedding and eager to learn what having a stepdad would be like. If he had done or said something to initiate our long-standing mutual dislike and mistrust, I couldn't remember. It may have been his disinterest in me as a child, or jealousy toward me for being the recipient of so much of my mom's attention. But was it my job as a seven-year-old to interpret that behavior as the once-necessary self-preserving defensiveness of a misunderstood man still wounded from his childhood? Or was it okay to hate someone who has chosen to be unkind to you, whatever the psychological reasoning? Maybe not. Maybe I owed it to him, or to my mom, or to myself, to try harder to like Seth. Could it be part of my personal journey to figure out how to love someone who didn't love me and who consistently made life harder for me and the people I loved? Or was that being a weak, spineless pushover? However I framed the question, the answer seemed more elusive.

One night after my mom and I got home from the hospital, I went to the computer to play a fish-tank simulation game that I was into. On the screen I saw an e-receipt for an ad on some kind of music-promotion website, obviously something Seth had bought to fuel his inevitable success as a performer. I knew that my mom would be upset if she knew about Seth's purchase, and that it would likely start a huge fight if I said anything.

I closed the window for the e-receipt and opened my fish game, saving my knowledge for some future unrelated fight between them, when the information might be used to overwhelm my mom into leaving her husband for good.

"I was using the computer," Seth said.

Seth and I fought over the computer like siblings. The unspoken house rule was that you could use the computer for as long as you wanted, but that if you got up to use the bathroom or make a snack, and someone else grabbed the computer while you were away, you lost out. Whether you were hand-coding a form poll about which Hanson song is the most emotional or researching new and inventive ways to waste the family's money, you lost out.

"Too bad," I said.

I fed my electronic fish over and over until they got sick and died.

•

I told my cousin Alana to download ICQ so I could chat with her. Then her mother, my aunt Lynn, started using ICQ as well, and then my mom, and then Seth.

For some reason my aunt Lynn garnered many dick pics from ICQ users, which she showed Alana and me. I covered my face, mortified that something like that would happen on a service I'd suggested to her.

"Here's another one," she said, laughing.

"You must be using ICQ wrong," I said.

"This is just how men are, Chelsea. Someday you'll understand."

My mom formed more intense relationships with people on ICQ. She talked to the same people on a daily basis. She sent these people boxes full of stuff she had purchased at Walmart.

"Why?" I asked.

"It's his son's birthday," she said.

"So?" I said. "It's a lot of people's birthdays. You don't normally send packages to random people for their birthday."

"I just want to, okay? It's none of your business. I'm my own person."

Maybe you should throw in some tea tree oil cleaners, I thought. *And leave the Crayolas here for me.*

One night I walked out of my bedroom to see my mom with her ear against the door to the garage. I looked at her inquisitively.

"Shh," she said.

I pressed my own ear against the door, and heard Seth's muffled voice. He was on the phone, speaking more gently and clearly than he usually did.

"I can't wait to meet you," I heard him say.

My mom whipped open the door and started screaming at Seth. Their fight moved around the house and into the driveway for all our neighbors to witness.

I gathered, from the things they were yelling at each other, that Seth had been speaking to a woman named Cherry, who he had begun chatting with on ICQ a few weeks before.

I didn't feel angry with Seth for being disloyal to my mom. I didn't consider my mom's feelings about the situation at all. I momentarily felt sorry for the woman named Cherry for being tricked into believing that Seth was someone worth talking to before realizing that she could be the one to set us free from him forever. She was a wedge in their marriage with real potential.

I considered bringing up my mom's foray into infidelity in the form of boxes of markers to a strange man's child. But even though the stakes were so high and the rewards for driving them apart so great, I didn't want to betray my mom.

"Maybe now is a good time to mention the receipt I saw on the computer last week for the ad you bought," I said.

"You little bitch," Seth said.

"Don't call her that," my mom said. She sounded noncommittally irritated, perhaps a little relieved that the fight had been directed away from her.

"Why?" he said. "She's a fucking little bitch. What were you doing? Spying on me like a little fucking creep?"

"What ad?" my mom said pathetically, pointlessly.

I went to my room and picked up a large cup of flat soda I had been neglecting to take to the kitchen sink for the last few days, carried it to the dining room, and threw the contents, as well as the cup itself, onto Seth.

He lunged at me, but I didn't move as he might have expected me to, and he had to stop himself to avoid crashing into me. I stood there hoping he would hit me, or spit on me, or do something else that was plainly unforgivable, that would force my mom to leave him, knowing, sadly, that he wouldn't. He was very good at riding the line between total piece of shit and passable human.

He theatrically flipped me off and returned to fighting with my mom, using my erratic behavior as fuel for his anger. Their fight devolved into the name-calling and stomping around that were becoming completely normal and comfortable for me to watch, and it was clear that this was just one of many fights, with many more to come.

"I'm not sure why she's acting like that," I heard my mom say to Seth hours later. "She's probably about to start her period."

5

A YEAR WITHOUT SPOONS

In October of my freshman year of high school, I switched schools. I was happy about the move, because I wasn't doing very well socially. I had a group of friends that I hung out with during lunch period and on some weekends, but each person in that group thought of me as their least important friend. I was ready to move on.

My mom had gotten a job long-term substitute teaching for a science class at Lower Lake High through the end of the year, and, aside from wanting to ditch my group of non-friends, I liked the idea of being driven to and from school every day.

Switching schools was kind of my thing. My family moved frequently during my childhood, but only ever to the next town or two towns over, so a lot of times I would be transferred back to a school I had already attended at some point. All my old friends and classmates would be there still, only three years older. I would be sort of the new girl, and sort of the girl who had disappeared for a while. I was terrible at making new friends, but even worse at picking up old friendships after long periods. I avoided the old friends I had fallen out of contact with as if we despised each other for some forgotten reason.

Seeing all my old classmates at Lower Lake High was like seeing into the future. Or the past, depending on your perspective. I could see remnants of their cute kid faces behind these older, less adorable, more awkwardly pubescent ones.

There was the boy from my kindergarten class who used to give himself hickeys on his arm when he was nervous or excited, now wearing hair gel and cologne and talking to girls without even sucking on his arm flesh.

There was my best friend from third grade, hanging out with the boy I picked on/had a crush on in fifth grade.

There was the girl who had punched me in the stomach when I told her I wanted her to play Pumbaa in our dance interpretation of *The Lion King* in fourth grade because she thought I was making a comment about her weight, hanging out with who I thought was the boy who used to nap during recess in first grade but who was actually a similar-looking kid from my third-grade class.

There was the boy who had made me cry several times in first grade by calling me "blue-eyed blondie," which I all of a sudden recognized may have been a compliment but which didn't matter anyway because now he was on the basketball team and that fact alone made him utterly intimidating.

I knew that these people recognized me, and I knew they knew that I recognized them, but, following that brief moment of recognition and almost simultaneous redirection of our eyes, we effectively communicated to each other that there was no interest in rekindling old friendships. As long as I diverted my eyes slightly before they did, I felt okay about this, as they would know that it was my decision not to talk.

There were also plenty of people I didn't recognize, kids who must have gone to the one elementary school in the area I had never attended, or kids who had moved here from elsewhere, but none of them immediately interested me either.

•

I had science class with my mom the period before lunch, and would stay and hang out with her until the bell rang. Sometimes she would sneak me off campus and we would go to McDonald's or run an errand. Otherwise we would eat cafeteria lunch in her classroom and she would tell me what her students had done or said in her classes that day.

My mom was young and cute, and a lot of her stories were about the junior and senior jocks flirting with her, asking if she was married and inviting her to hang out with them on the weekend.

Sometimes, she said, these same boys asked about me.

"Me?" I would say, confounded.

"Yeah. They're amazed I have a daughter as old as you."

"Oh."

"Why don't you be friends with Naema?" my mom said a few months into the school year. "She's pretty cool. Her family moved here from Arizona. She has a brother who is River's age."

Naema was a girl I talked to in Art and P.E. and we sometimes ate lunch together. She was new that year, so I had an advantage over her in knowing insignificant details about some of our classmates' childhoods, which seemed to impress her or at least hold her attention.

I had thought I *was* becoming friends with Naema, but my mom's implication that I wasn't yet friends with her, along with her assumption that I didn't know where she had moved from, as well as her apparent belief that I couldn't decide who to be friends with on my own, insulted me and undermined the very reason, in my opinion, to have friends in the first place, which is to have a life separate from the one your parents know about.

I didn't want to be friends with someone who was friendly with my mom. I didn't want to watch what I said around either of them, to worry about them speaking casually with each other.

I couldn't imagine telling Naema not to talk to my mom, because I didn't want to appear controlling, and also because I didn't want my mom's feelings to be hurt if she found out. And I didn't want to tell my mom to stop talking to Naema because I thought she wouldn't stop anyway, and it would become a shared joke between my mom and Naema that they weren't supposed to talk to me. I simply stopped speaking to Naema.

Naema barely seemed to notice.

I accepted that I might never have friends again. Having spent most of my life being the new girl, I had never really "made friends" so much as attached myself to the first person who showed mild interest in me. Whether they liked me or not, they were stuck with me. I decided that I wasn't going to do that anymore. I wasn't going to approach *anyone*. I wasn't going to pursue friendship of any kind. If someone wanted to be friends with me, they were going to have to work really hard to prove it to me.

Once I decided to stop making any attempt to appear nonpathetic, I felt liberated. I stopped hanging out with my mom during lunch and fully embraced my lonerdom. I raced to my favorite bench when the lunch bell rang so I could spread my things over it and make it awkward for anyone else to try to sit near me.

I started wearing bright blue eye shadow up to my eyebrows and raver pants and tight, brightly colored tank tops and T-shirts. I wore neon miniskirts with torn, filthy, giant hoodies and metallic combat boots. I wore skimpy tank tops over my little brother's old sports T-shirts with plaid bell-bottoms and suspenders and a velveteen blazer. Nobody else dressed this way, and I wasn't sure if I was being judged or not, but I decided I didn't care. If all it took to be disliked was weird fashion, an off-putting personality, and a commitment to disregarding what anyone thought about me, then I didn't want to be liked.

"Everyone tells me they think you're cool and mysterious," my mom said. I believed her, because people had started approaching me to compliment me on my colorful accessories and interesting hairstyles. My preemptive rejection of my classmates had given me a new kind of confidence, almost a cockiness. I was trying to gain control over the reasons people didn't like me by manufacturing more reasons for them to not like me, but the reasons I was manufacturing had turned into reasons for them to like me.

One thing was becoming very clear: I did not understand people.

Some of my classmates began sitting with me on my bench. Sometimes talking to me and sometimes not. Sometimes I would engage them and sometimes I wouldn't. Sometimes I would ignore a person who was talking directly to me. Sometimes I would talk to a person as naturally as I could manage and then, later, after the bell rang, would whisper, "Why won't you just leave me alone?" loud enough for that person to hear as they walked away from me.

Essentially, I was a bitch. A bitch who didn't care that she was a bitch, but who believed she was cool or mysterious enough to compensate for her bitchiness, but who nevertheless had no friends.

I was a lonely little bitch.

It was hard to admit I was lonely. Part of my new identity was accepting being alone without feeling lonely, though I guessed accepting loneliness could be incorporated into my new antisocial personality.

I began making "classtime friends," who were people I would talk to and hang out with during class but avoid during break times.

A "classtime friend" named Jake, who had the beginnings of a mustache and who I had a crush on, asked me out between fourth and fifth period.

I said very slowly and clearly, "I'm going to pretend I didn't hear that," and walked away from him. I had never had a boyfriend, and knew I could not manage all the first experiences that come with having one without a girl friend to talk things through with.

He asked me out again at the same time the next day and I said,

"Look, fine. But we're not ever going to hang out, you can't tell anyone we're going out, and I'm not giving you my phone number."

He agreed, but then stopped talking to me completely, and I spent the next few months being in love with him from afar. It was very romantic.

I stopped using spoons one day. I was becoming weird, I knew. And it didn't seem like the good kind of weird, like the eccentric arty weird that could be appreciated by other people. It seemed like the bad, dark kind that could unravel a person if it got out of hand. Was this a cry for help? A desperate, attention-seeking maneuver? Because if so, no one really noticed. It was just my own silverware rule that affected pretty much no one, myself included. It was one minor, meaningless limitation of my own making, in a world full of uncontrollable limitations.

No spoons.

"I'm not using spoons anymore," I announced to my mom. I had gone several days without using spoons before I said something, just to make sure I could do it.

"What about cereal?" my mom said.

I raised an eyebrow. Aha. I would have to stop eating cereal. Cereal was a food I ate once in a while, and now it was out of the question.

A desperate, attention-seeking maneuver that affects no one, huh? I thought sarcastically toward my own inner monologue. *We'll see how long you last without a food you occasionally enjoy.*

Your life is a disaster, my inner monologue shot back, laughing. I ate cereal with a fork with pretty much no problem.

The drive to and from school with my mom took close to an hour. I made mixtapes to listen to on the drive and became irritated when my mom tried to talk to me. I wanted to hear the same songs, over and over, completely undisturbed, until we got to school.

I began having a hard time making conversation with my mom. Nothing felt different, but I couldn't remember how to talk to her. I couldn't believe it had ever been easy, because now it felt so difficult and complicated. I didn't have anything to say. All of my thoughts were extremely confidential.

If she noticed this change, she didn't say anything, and I didn't notice her noticing it.

My mom's curriculum included tending a vegetable garden adjacent to her classroom. She brought my Polaroid camera to school and took photos of her students with the plants they were growing. I was mortified, as I felt sure that everyone thought that the whole "Polaroid photos in the garden" thing was part of a perverted ploy for my mom to get pictures of boys so I could hang them on my bedroom wall, which I did.

"What boys do you like?" my mom would ask.

I thought of all the boys I had crushes on, and chose the one who I least cared about.

"Corey," I would say, "is kind of cute, I guess."

Corey was the first but not the last boy I had a crush on who I later found out was in the special education program.

Daniel was a cute, popular senior. He was really dumb, and mean, in a way that only cute, popular, really dumb boys could get away with. He would have completely blended into the faceless mass of "cool" older boys, except for the fact that he regularly teased me.

"Nice bangs, Mrs. Johnson's daughter," he would say, laughing. Before I had time to respond, he would begin to saunter away from me, as if he had somewhere to go but had a really long time to get there.

I hated him. I hated the way he talked, as if everything he said was some big joke that no one else was in on. I hated that people liked him. I hated that he thought he could talk to me. And I hated that he was so cute, because it complicated the situation, made it slightly exciting that he had chosen me to pick on and/or be weird to (or whatever was happening).

When he was close by I would prepare myself to react to whatever he might say to me with the appropriate blend of annoyance, indifference, and social ineptitude, which was the recipe for my newfound personal brand.

Many times, though, he wouldn't approach or speak to me, and I would direct the annoyance, indifference, and social ineptitude inward, reproach myself for expecting Daniel to talk to me or wanting anything to do with him, and for hating him and wanting his attention simultaneously.

Though I felt pretty lonely most of the day at school, I loved being alone in my bedroom. There was nothing better than shutting my door, turning the music up really loud, and spending hours doing vaguely creative small projects. I made conceptual mixtapes, including one with only the grunts and superfluous *ooh*s and *oh yeah*s from my favorite albums. I wrote out the lyrics of my favorite songs on scraps of paper and memorized them. I glued soda bottle caps to my backpack. I stapled old mousepads and photos and ribbon and all kinds of garbage to my walls to make a hideous 3-D collage. I ripped advertisements for alcohol or perfume out of *Rolling Stone* and *Cosmo* and re-created the ads in acrylic paint on canvas. I printed images of musicians I found on the internet onto T-shirt transfer paper and ironed the images onto my clothing.

I knew I had something to say, but I didn't trust myself to find the right way to say it yet. I took other people's words and images and tried to find a way for them to fit me.

I never thought of what I was doing as art, or even self-expression. I never went out of my way to show anyone what I made or did. Though a lot of the output of my efforts was truly bad, it was, looking back, the purest form of creativity I've ever known, free of pretension or ego and completely absorbed by itself and its own influences.

I didn't need anybody to tell me what was good or bad or worthy of my time. The more time I spent alone in my room, the more this fact slowly began informing my self-image. I was the sole judge of what was cool or interesting or worth thinking about.

I didn't need anybody.

"I was a loner when I was your age, too," my mom said.

She was full of shit. I knew she'd had friends because she had maintained friendships with the girls she was friends with at my age. I had met them. I had heard them talking about the wild adventures they had when they were my age. Plus she got pregnant with me when she was seventeen, which required, I assumed, at least passable social skills.

"No, I really was," she said. "I would go to parties and sit in the corner and read a book and all of my friends would be like, *What are you doing reading that book? Come dance!*"

The last party I had been to was a birthday party almost two years earlier, where I accidentally admitted I liked the band Aqua when everyone was talking about a rapper who had a song with a similar-sounding title, and everyone had looked around at one another like, *This moron thinks we're talking about "Barbie Girl."*

"I don't think it counts as being a loner if you got invited to parties and your friends were upset that you weren't hanging out with them enough."

"You'll get invited to parties. You're just at an awkward age."

I wanted to believe her. I'd had friends just a couple of years before, after all. I'd gotten invited to sleepovers, been asked to promise my allegiance to insecure friends, regularly knocked on the bedroom windows of people from school at 1 a.m. and been greeted with enthusiasm. I had done these things easily, unfazed by how I was being perceived. Now I was fourteen and everything had changed.

Fourteen, I thought, shaking my head in agreement with myself. *You tricky bitch.*

But quickly I remembered all the fourteen-year-olds I knew at school—the ones who had sex with one another and skipped class to get drunk with their older boyfriends. Or the ones who brought their guitars to school to show their friends what they had practiced the night before. Or the ones who were able to hold conversations with their adult science teacher while posing for Polaroids in the garden. Or even the ones who got together during lunch hour to quiz each other about vocabulary words.

It wasn't the age that was awkward. I was awkward. My mom was trying to make me believe I was normal, that my age was to blame for my complete social ineptness, but I wasn't normal. There was no guarantee I would ever have friends again.

"I'm sorry," she said. "This is my fault. I should have been more social when you were growing up."

I tried to imagine a reality in which, because my mom was social while I was growing up, I did not turn into the strange loner freak that I was. It would be nice to have some outside force to blame, but in some ways it was even more comforting, in the way things become comforting through habit, to blame only myself.

At least the spoon thing was going well. I counted off the days as if I were a recovering alcoholic. Fifteen days without spoons . . . Four months without spoons . . . Five months without using spoons, and ten days since I accidentally touched a spoon when carelessly grabbing a fork from the dishwasher.

If the spoon thing was a cry for help, it was a weak, internal cry. I knew it probably signified something sad and desperate about my personality. The spoon thing, the assignment of the slightest, dumbest handicap to myself, was a reminder that I was both in control and out of control, that I could force myself to behave a certain way for months on end, for no reason, that I was that easy for my own self to manipulate.

This is so stupid, I would think, and the thought would immediately be followed by *But, alas, this is who I've chosen to be.*

I was trying to gain dominance over myself as a way to prove that there was a difference between my intentions and my actions, as a way to prove I was not really who it was starting to seem like I was.

The spoon thing, of course, wasn't who I was. It was like a fake lip ring or an ill-advised pair of suspenders, an accessory to compensate for my actual personality, a disguise to conceal the flaws I didn't know how to address. It was a distraction from my real personality defects, something I could identify as the source of my "weirdness" and my problems, but that was actually a symptom of the larger problems I did not want to deal with.

Also, it made it really hard to eat school hot lunch, because the cafeteria only offered sporks, which I had decided counted as a spoon three days into my spoon thing.

I made friends with three Mexican girls. One of them, Angelica, was assigned to be my partner in English class, and she told me she would find me at lunch so we could finish our history assignment. She found me on my bench and ate with me. Then she asked me to follow her to the locker room, where her two best friends were hanging out.

I talked with Angelica most days in class, and sometimes I abandoned my bench to hang out with them in the locker room. I was hoping to become close enough to them that I would have people to hang out with during summer break, which was fast approaching. They mostly spoke Spanish, unless they had something to say directly to me, which meant I didn't have to listen to their conversations unless someone said my name first, which I thought was neat. They were big on cute little nicknames, and they called me Chelso.

"Chelso, there's your boyfriend," Angelica said, pointing to Jake, the boy I had agreed to date months earlier and hadn't talked to since. They all laughed and said something in Spanish and then lightly pushed me on the arm, the way close-knit teenage girls did in tampon commercials. I avoided eye contact with Jake and saw from the corner of my eye that he was avoiding eye contact with me.

"Did that Jake guy ask you out?" my mom said.

"No," I said. "How did you know that?"

"He's in my third period."

Maybe he was in her third period, but there was no way he'd volunteered that information to my mom. I looked at her suspiciously.

"Did Angelica tell you?" I said.

"Jake is really sweet. I like his sideburns."

"Mrs. Johnson's daughter, will you go to prom with me?" Daniel said to me on our midmorning break.

"Yeah," I said. I hadn't meant to respond so quickly, or in the affirmative. But what else do you say to the cute, popular idiot who is perpetually making you feel like you're not in on some hilarious joke that is most likely being made at your expense, when he asks you to be his prom date?

You say no, my inner monologue reminded me, *because he sucks and you hate him and probably no one has ever put him in his place.*

My quick "yeah" was confirmation that there was some part of me that wanted Daniel to accept me and make me cool and popular, like him. That I wanted him to sweep me away on prom night and convince me, over the course of the evening, that he was misunderstood, that his good looks caused a lot of personality problems for him and that he was trying to identify and overcome those problems, and that he wanted me to be part of that journey with him.

Daniel sauntered away from me toward his laughing male posse, confirming my suspicion that I was the butt of a poorly conceived, mean-spirited joke, or that this was a medium-pathetic way for Daniel to gauge his own popularity.

"I'll try to remember to go," I yelled, exposing my desperate need to appear indifferent.

I stood in the courtyard with a blank expression, trying to figure out if I appeared unaffected or deeply affected, then wondered if it made any difference to anyone which one I appeared to be, and then considered which feeling I was actually feeling, then considered what I appeared to be feeling now, to people who saw me standing in the middle of the courtyard by myself for over a minute, then looked around to see who might be wondering about my feelings about standing in the courtyard, then checked back in with myself to see what my feelings were.

Still not sure, I thought.

The second bell rang while I stood there, indicating that I was late to class.

Let's kick this spoon thing up a notch, my inner monologue said.

I had gone without spoons for eight months, and I barely gave it a thought anymore. It didn't feel like a restriction anymore. I needed to make it laborious again.

Knives could be an interesting utensil to live without. How would I cut things? Or spread them? Going without both knives and spoons could pose some interesting challenges. I could overcome those challenges by refusing to see them as challenges and instead calling them "accomplishments."

Maybe these "accomplishments" could shed some light on what kind of person I wanted to be, because I obviously couldn't figure that out on my own.

Maybe I could stop using kitchen utensils of any kind and prepare and eat all my food with my fingers.

Maybe eating with my fingers would be less gimmicky and more authentic. A punk-rock eff-you to institutionalized utensil implementation.

No, I thought confidently, maybe a little sternly. *This is where I draw the line.*

By the end of the year, students started ditching their classes to hang out in my mom's science room/garden. There would be no more class work, she decided, only gardening and socializing. She left the door to the classroom and the door to the garden open. Bright summer light streamed in from both sides of the room and students drifted in and out of the classroom. Teachers of neighboring classrooms began to complain about the noise, but my mom didn't change her policies.

A student stepped on one of the class computers while dancing on top of a desk and my mom hid the broken computer under some boxes of barely used microscopes so that the school administration wouldn't find it until the year was over and she was no longer responsible for the science equipment.

"Just try to be cool," she pleaded with her students. "The year is almost over."

Daniel and the other jocks asked my mom what she was doing for the summer, and invited her to ride Sea-Doos with them on the lake. My mom happily agreed and told them to call her, but she didn't give them our phone number.

I wondered if Daniel was trying to get my mom's number as a means to reach me, or if he was attempting to get me to fall in love with him as a means to reach my mom, or if he was constructing a false reality purely to confuse and manipulate me, or if my mom had convinced him to flirt with her so that I would assume he was trying to get to me so that I might feel desirable, or if he wasn't doing anything except being talkative and outgoing, and that his attractiveness was making me project flirtation onto everything he did.

I didn't go to prom with Daniel. It was a joke, obviously. I had never had any misconception that it was anything other than a big, hilarious joke that I was definitely in on the entire time.

That summer, someone handed me a bowl of ice cream with a spoon sticking out of it, like a dare. The spoon seemed forbidden and exotic to me, and I felt an urge to rebel. Rebel against myself, I guess, or rebel against the things I had convinced myself were important but were actually pointless, or rebel against the fork industry, which I had inadvertently aligned myself with and was now regretting.

But I had been clean and spoonless for ten months, and I was proud of that. It was stupid, I knew that, but it meant something to me. It meant I was capable. I had decided to do something and, despite the many bumps and twists in logic I had to employ along the way, I had done it. I had succeeded at something. Giving it up because I was embarrassed to admit who I was would be a step backward.

I slowly brought a spoonful of ice cream up to my mouth and licked it, not touching the spoon with my tongue.

6

VOLUNTARY RESPONSES TO INVOLUNTARY SENSATIONS

The hill man first came to me while I was in my bed one night, a detail-less 2-D hallucination. The hill man walked up the hill until he reached a medium-size rock about three-quarters of the way up. The hill man stumbled over the rock, fell down to the bottom of the hill, picked himself up, and started walking up the hill again, where he again stumbled on the same rock, fell down the hill in the same way, and again started walking up the hill. It was like a very boring 8-bit video game, and it lulled me to sleep within an hour.

I thought of the hill man for most of the next day, while making self-portraits in acrylic on tiny canvas boards in my room. The hill man's journey up the hill had no beginning and no end. By the end of the day I had thought of him (with varying degrees of focus) for almost ten full hours, and he still had not made it up the hill without stumbling over the rock.

Same thing the next day.

Same thing the day after that.

As far as unwanted repetitive thoughts went, this wasn't so bad, contentwise. For as long as I could remember, after thoughts like *I'm feeling great*, or *I'm having fun*, my mind compulsively listed all the things I regretted most in my life: *Ruined my mom's childhood doll on purpose. Faked tears when my great-grandma died.* When someone of authority talked to me, I would often think, *Don't kiss her, don't kiss her, don't kiss her,* until the authority figure stopped talking to me. But the hill man was far and away the most persistent unwanted thought I had ever had.

One night in bed, after a couple of solid weeks with the hill man, I concentrated intently on his journey. I believed that if he made his way over the rock and to the top of the hill, I could finally stop thinking about him. But my brain was stuck in a loop. Over and over and over, the hill man stumbled over the rock. I laughed a little in my bed in the dark, thinking that I was just pretending I could not control my imagination. Then I redoubled my efforts and tried again. I zoomed in to focus on just the man, the way his legs moved, carefully guiding his foot over and to the other side of the rock. But it wouldn't work. He always tripped. I had no control.

I felt at odds with my mind, as if it were a separate entity from myself. It was like I had been tricked my whole life into thinking I had the ability to think whatever I wanted, and was suddenly given concrete proof that I did not have that control. I could not imagine the man going up the hill without stumbling, nor could I will him and his pointless journey out of my mind.

The hill man remained with me in some form for almost all waking hours. Sometimes I would lazily let the images play in my mind, not trying to control the hill man at all. Other times I would concentrate deeply, trying to help him overcome the imaginary rock that now seemed like one of my biggest problems in life.

The neck thing was the same but different. It began several weeks after the hill man. I flexed the left side of my neck, causing my head to turn to the left slightly. I didn't know why I was doing this. There was no reason for it. It didn't feel particularly good.

In theory, I had total control over the movements of my body. The neck thing wasn't a spasm. I performed the neck flex just as I would perform the series of movements necessary to scratch an itch. It wasn't unconscious. It was deliberate. But, then again, not twitching my neck made me feel uncomfortable, just as leaving an itch unscratched would. I wanted to flex my neck. I couldn't stop thinking about wanting to flex my neck. I simply had to flex my neck. So I did. Sometimes this would satisfy me (but was it really me who was being satisfied?) and sometimes it wouldn't. Sometimes I had to flex my neck multiple times to feel satisfied. Sometimes dozens.

I didn't know how visible my neck tic was, but I wanted to keep people from seeing it. I would pretend to itch my ear, cover my neck muscle with my hand, or put my hood up. Sometimes I would excuse myself to the bathroom and flex as hard as I could, trying to satisfy the urge.

I didn't want to tell anybody. I had never heard anyone describe the persistent unwanted thoughts and uncontrollable body movements I was experiencing. It would sound freakish to explain that I could not stop imagining a man trying to climb a hill, even though I didn't want to imagine it and the thought wasn't interesting, and that the man couldn't even climb the hill all the way, and that I was obsessed with getting myself to imagine him making it up the hill all the way, even though, as previously mentioned, I did not care. And the neck thing, which was possibly related, possibly worse, possibly even less logical: an insatiable need to jerk my head around unnaturally, especially in front of people I did not want to notice me.

These could only be symptoms of something very bad, I thought. A personality disorder. The beginning of my psychotic breakdown.

Eventually I told my mom. I tried to approach the subject delicately, as I didn't want her to think I was crazy.

"It's silly but I can't stop thinking about it," I said, describing the man on the hill. "Sometimes I think about him for hours."

"Have you tried doing anything to relax?" my mom asked. "Like massaging your temples or deep breathing?"

"I've tried, but I just think about him even while I'm doing that stuff. It's like I don't have control over my own mind. Also, I keep doing this thing with my neck. Like, flexing my neck muscles. I'm afraid people can see it and my neck is always sore."

My mom picked me up from school one day and took me to the doctor, and the doctor referred me to a neurologist.

"I think about this man who walks up a hill and then falls down. He does it over and over, and he never makes it up the hill because there's a rock that he trips over. Once I start thinking about him, I can do it for hours. I picture him going up the hill, tripping, falling, and then going back up the hill over and over."

"Those sound like some pretty intrusive thoughts," the neurologist said.

"And then, I don't know if it's related," I said, "but I have to move my neck a certain way, sometimes over and over. It doesn't feel right unless I do it the right way. Even if I do it the right way, sometimes I still have to do it a bunch of times."

"What happens if you don't do it?"

"If I don't do it I can't focus on anything else. I just keep thinking about how I want to flex my neck."

"Have you read *The Man Who Mistook His Wife for a Hat*?" the neurologist asked, looking at my mom. With the attention off me, I took a moment to scan the room. The office seemed plain and notably un-brain-doctory. I expected an X-ray of a brain or something on the wall, or plastic models of brains scattered across well-loved bookshelves. There was nothing on the walls but the neurologist's diploma. There were no bookshelves or decorations or even a rug. Just a desk and three chairs.

"No, I haven't," my mom said.

"Oliver Sacks is the author," he said. "It's a must-read. There is a chapter about Tourette's syndrome. The way Oliver Sacks writes is just remarkable. The whole book is astounding."

I don't want to read a book, I thought angrily while nodding politely. *I want you to tell me what to do.*

"Tourette's syndrome?" my mom said. "Is that what you think Chelsea has?"

"It sounds like Tourettic tics," he said. "With some obsessive-compulsive tendencies that are causing the intrusive thoughts," he said, writing something on a pad of paper, which he then handed to me. *The Man Who Mistook His Wife for a Hat*, it read. Then he picked up his prescription pad and wrote me a prescription for a low-dosage antipsychotic.

Tourette's syndrome and *obsessive-compulsive disorder* were definitely terms I wanted to keep hidden. I'd rather people think I was making erratic movements for no reason than for a reason that made me sound mentally ill. They were terms that were misunderstood or barely understood, both by me and by the culture at large, and I didn't want to be associated with them. I also believed they weren't the correct diagnosis. I hadn't expressed clearly that I was in control of the neck movements. That it was the compulsion to do these things that was out of my control, not the actions themselves. If I focused hard and used all my willpower, I could prevent myself from performing the movements.

And the hill man. I still didn't believe it was anything more than me being weird, my attention-seeking personality tricking myself into believing I couldn't control the outcome of a thought.

I blamed myself for describing my symptoms unclearly.

At the same time, the terms also soothed me. I wanted them to be mine. If there were names for what I was experiencing, that meant my strange and embarrassing behaviors were at least common enough to have been identified, which meant there were other people who did the same kinds of things, which meant maybe this wasn't my fault, that maybe fault existed somewhere outside the realm of my responsibility. Deep in my brain, some mysterious synapse was misfiring, the whole system inaccessible to my conscious desire not to do weird shit.

I had no idea what the drugs were supposed to do to me, so all summer I looked for changes of any kind. Did I feel calmer? Did I have less physical energy? Were my thoughts changing? Was I able to control my imagination more effectively? Could I remain still for any length of time at all?

The only thing I noticed was that I developed new tics in my left breast and biceps. They ticced in sequence with my neck: *neck, breast, biceps, neck, breast, biceps*. An internal percussion that my body subtly but visibly swayed to. After a few days of medication, a tic in my left calf muscle was added to the progression, followed shortly by a tic in my left buttock. These additions were actually a relief to my neck, because it increased the time between each tic of my neck, which was becoming more and more strained from so much flexing.

I could still stop the tics at any time, but it took all of my concentration. I could sit and not tic, but I had to think *Don't tic, don't tic, just wait, don't do it*, and the second I stopped focusing on it, I would let go and the chorus of tics would begin.

I purposefully conjured up the image of the hill man. Maybe now that I was on these drugs, I could get him over the rock and all the way up the hill. At the top of the hill I wanted there to be a precipice, which I would make him walk out onto before falling off to meet his everlasting death.

I focused hard on conjuring these images. I was determined to beat him. But the man was trapped in the same old cycle. He walked up the hill. He didn't seem to see the rock. He tripped over it. Stumbled down. Walked up again. Tripped on the rock.

I keep slipping, I thought, just like the hill man. We are both destined to carry out the same meaningless activities eternally. It will never end because no ending exists. There is nothing after the rock except the beginning of the hill.

I made a careful effort to watch myself tic, trying to find the root cause. I wasn't telling my biceps to flex, the way I would "tell" my arm to move if I was lighting a candle or pressing a button. And it wasn't quite like an itch: my muscles did not feel particularly unsatisfied before the tic, nor did they feel satisfied afterward. If I focused on not flexing my biceps, I could avoid ticcing, but once I stopped focusing, it would tic freely, like a child just waiting for its parent to look away to do something bad.

Was my mind broken in two? Did I have a second mind that was at odds with the first mind? Was it the mind of a naughty child in search of new ways to be bad? How long had this problem been developing? Did it really just appear overnight, as it seemed?

Maybe I had been ticcing and obsessively entertaining pointless thoughts for years, only I was too focused on other things to notice.

Soon it was September, and I had to go back to school. My embarrassing and unexplainable tics disincentivized making friends, as without friends I did not have to hide my weird movements from anyone. In class, I would try to sit in the back corner, where no one could see me without turning around in their chairs. In classes in which I was assigned seating in front of other desks, I spent all my energy trying not to tic.

For the first time in my life, I found it hard to concentrate at school. I was completely preoccupied with the length and nuance of my tics, and with hiding the visibility of the tics from my classmates, and, when I had all of that under control, on the hill man's progress up the increasingly important hill. If I could just get him over the rock and up the hill, maybe I could regain control of my body.

Because it had been so long since I'd had a friend, or perhaps because I had believed myself to be a freak for so long, someone who would never be understood by other people, I became more and more comfortable with being the "social outcast" type. I became depressed, and sort of enjoyed it. I listened to the Smiths and the Cure alone in my dark bedroom and counted all the ways I was alone. *Night after night she lay alone in bed, / her eyes so open to the dark.*

The music and lyrics conveyed bleakness and depression and hopelessness, which were things I related to, but they did not express *exactly* what I was feeling, so therefore they represented yet another reason I was utterly alone in the world, which was perfect.

In class I stared at all the people who weren't as fucked up or complicated as I was, feeling superior for it. I also felt sick of feeling superior, and wasn't buying into my own delusion anymore. What the fuck made me superior anyway? My childish disdain for anyone who didn't automatically like me? How original. But what could I do? I was trapped in my malfunctioning body, whose only defense mechanism was to feel superior and shut everyone out. I recalled my favorite lyrics to make myself feel sad in just the particular way I was used to, and became calm: *I'm running towards nothing / again and again and again and again.*

"Are there other treatment options?" my mom asked the neurologist during my next visit. "Chelsea doesn't like the risperidone or however you say it."

"We can try something else, sure," he said. "Oh, and before I forget, I wanted to recommend you both read *The Man Who Mistook His Wife for a Hat* by Oliver Sacks. It's really great."

"Oh yeah. You mentioned that last time," my mom said. "We haven't read it yet." It was like my neurologist had a particular strain of obsessive-compulsive disorder that caused him to recommend *The Man Who Mistook His Wife for a Hat* to his patients repeatedly.

"The man who has Tourette's syndrome in that book tries medication, but he ultimately finds that the medications dull his mind and leave him a shadow of what he was with the Tourette's, so he stops taking meds and lives with Tourette's syndrome."

"It dulled his mind?" I asked.

"You'll have to read the book," the neurologist said.

"I'm in control of what I'm doing," I said, trying to be assertive. "The tics, I mean. I'm physically doing them. My muscles aren't just spasming on their own. I can stop doing it if I really concentrate on it. So is that Tourette's still?"

"Yes. Sometimes patients with Tourette's syndrome are able to suppress their symptoms, but will usually feel a build-up of pressure or need to perform the action of their tic," he said.

"Yeah," I said.

He was describing my exact experience, but I still felt unsure about my diagnosis, hesitant to believe him, convinced that I had not expressed myself clearly or conveyed my experience accurately. And the drugs weren't working. So clearly there was some kind of problem.

I developed a new tic in my abdomen. This tic was superior to all previous tics, because it didn't need to be a part of the chorus of other tics, sustained itself for up to thirty seconds at a time, and could be performed at the same time as any of my other tics. It would be *neck, breast, biceps, calf, buttock, neck, breast, biceps, calf, buttock*, and all the while my abdomen would be flexed. Soon, the quick flexing of my other tics wasn't satisfying either, and they became sustained as well, and huge areas of my body flexed simultaneously for up to ten seconds at a time.

The abdomen tic evolved to include a small, controlled exhale that sounded like *hut*, which transformed into a series of small, controlled exhales that sounded like *hut, hut, hut, hut*. It was the first time I was doing something audible, and, though it was pretty quiet, it couldn't easily be covered up.

I know what you're doing, I told myself, not knowing at all what I was doing and not sure who I thought I was addressing, *and it's not going to work*.

I believed, or wanted to believe, or thought it would be most indicative of good mental health to believe, that I was doing all of this to myself. That I was trying to get attention. That I had nothing to offer the world so I was making up symptoms to seem more interesting. That I had successfully tricked my mom and the neurologist into believing I had a disorder, even though that disorder was previously unknown to me, all the while, deep inside, knowing that it was all a game. A sick, weird, mentally unstable game. If anything, my disease was being able to conjure symptoms of a disease I'd had no idea existed, and convince everyone that I had that disease.

"Have I told you about *The Man Who Mistook His Wife for a Hat*?" the neurologist said. I looked behind me as people do on sitcoms to mean *Are you talking to me? / Is this some kind of joke?* Maybe recommending the same book over and over was some kind of subversive method of treatment. Maybe I was supposed to become so perplexed that my body would reroute the energy it spent on tics toward rolling my eyes and moaning in agony.

"I think so," I said. "And I think I want to go off the meds."

The neurologist stared at me, and I imagined he was trying to gauge how dull my mind had gotten.

"We could try a different prescription," he said. "There are lots of options."

"I don't know. It's not getting any better," I said. "And I don't like being on drugs."

My tics were, in fact, getting worse, more numerous, harder to control, and increasingly impossible to hide. I seemed to be developing new tics weekly, the most recent of which was to open my eyes very wide and look quickly to the right and left, as if I felt a sudden bolt of surprise and paranoia approximately eighty times per day. I had begun waking up with aching muscles. It was becoming more and more difficult to imagine that I had any power over the tics at all.

I wanted it to stop. I wanted it all to stop.

But more than wanting it to stop, I wanted to stop thinking about it. Between having tics and thinking about my tics and hiding my tics and trying to stop my tics and blaming myself for having tics and accusing myself of fabricating the whole tic situation and going to the neurologist to describe my tics and taking little pills that did nothing for my tics, I was doing little else. I simply wanted it to stop.

Maybe I couldn't stop all of it, but I could stop some of it.

I bought *The Man Who Mistook His Wife for a Hat* years later, after I'd had my abdomen tic so long that I was maintaining six-pack abs with zero effort. I loved the book, and it opened my eyes to the subtleties and complexities of the brain. There were a massive number of things that could go wrong, so many unknowns, so many strange connections. It is strangely comforting to realize that science is so far from identifying all the things that could go wrong in just one part of the human body.

I realized the hill man was gone one day. I hadn't thought about him in weeks. As soon as I stopped making an effort to obliterate him, it seemed, he started to go away on his own.

The hill man was replaced by other meaningless unwanted thoughts. For example, a boring loop of a dull conversation I had with a friend ten months before and suddenly remembered. Mentally listing every present ever given to me by my grandpa. Rolling and rerolling imaginary Yahtzee dice and never getting Yahtzee.

Over time, my tics got better and then they got worse and then much better and then much worse, a cycle that promises no end.

7

GOTH RYAN

My first thought when I met Goth Ryan was that he looked like the corpse of Macaulay Culkin, only skinnier. He was pale and wore a black trench coat and talked about *The Crow* a lot, and, though it might seem like a contradiction, he was also blond, smiley, and outgoing. He had sickly, sunken eye sockets and a high voice that broke when he became excited. Listening to him squeak through a conspiracy theory about the death of Brandon Lee, I realized I was attracted to him.

I mean, of course I was attracted to him. I had encountered very few male teenagers that I hadn't entertained perverted thoughts about. I was at that age, I guess, when even corpses made me horny.

But there were so many obstacles to our love. For one: he professed his love for me several times, very soon after I met him, which I saw as a red flag as well as a sign of questionable taste. Secondly: once, I saw his ex-girlfriend in Walmart and she screamed at me to stop fucking her boyfriend, and, though I was excited by the idea that anyone would assume I was fucking anyone, she kind of terrified me. Thirdly, and maybe most important: Goth Ryan was having some kind of secret sex affair with my best friend, Marcy. (It was secret because she had a boyfriend.)

Marcy had picked me to be her new best friend a few months earlier. The prior school year I'd had no friends or friend prospects and figured my sophomore year would be the same. Then one day in gym class, Marcy ditched her until-then best friend to walk laps around the field with me. We discussed the merits and flaws of Hot Topic, our current favorite bands (mine was Smashing Pumpkins, hers was Dashboard Confessional), how much we missed Napster, and the many idiots we went to school with. She invited me over to her house that night, and we dyed our hair pink with Manic Panic. She was not like me; she was loud and made offensive jokes and lived comfortably in the assumption that everyone found her charming. I immediately loved her.

I abandoned my desire to be alone at all times to do everything with Marcy: spending my lunch period in the snack bar next to her, filling Cup Noodles with hot water as a favor to the snack bar lady, who was a friend of Marcy's family; going to her house after school to make dinner with her grandma; staying up all night to console her about her tumultuous relationship and fight about which stand-up comedians were funnier.

Marcy's boyfriend introduced us to Goth Ryan, and the four of us hung out almost every weekend and on many school nights. Goth Ryan and Marcy's boyfriend were eighteen and had cars, so we would drive around blasting System of a Down until we found a quiet park with no tweakers in it to sit and drink. The three of them were almost certainly taking drugs of some kind, but I was never told what drugs, and somehow had no curiosity about it.

Alcohol, on the other hand. Big fan. Marcy's boyfriend and Goth Ryan always picked us up bearing disgusting bottles of Watermelon Schnapps or Hot Damn that I would never have picked out but that I drank greedily, often becoming blackout drunk. Once I was completely debilitated, Goth Ryan would wrap his trench coat around me and melodramatically promise me that everything would be okay, and that he would take care of me.

"Can I kiss you?" he sometimes said, nailing a tone of wilted theatrical romance, his black lips and eyes already betraying the pain of expecting rejection. It was pretty cute.

"Okay," I would say, trying to summon the strength to lift my head. Depending on variables completely unknown to me, Marcy would give me either a sexy/approving look or a pissed/jealous look, and, depending on my fluctuating hormones and levels of patience with her, I would either care or not care about whichever look she was giving me.

Marcy and I were impressed by the goth subculture Goth Ryan and Marcy's boyfriend took part in: not just the black strappy clothes, black fingernails, and heavy eye makeup (which we immediately began imitating), but also the directness and openness about feelings of sadness and inner rottenness. I usually felt ashamed of my unhappiness, and always cried in the shower where no one could hear me or ask me what I was crying about or tell me to stop. But these people were cutting themselves in places that couldn't easily be hidden, where others would see it and know that it was meant for them to see. There was something so powerful about that.

If Marcy and her boyfriend were fighting, we would hang out with other boys: Gabe, the much older Incubus fan; Tyler, the dweeby boy who would sometimes find us between classes and awkwardly give us drawings of various *Looney Tunes* characters that clearly had been traced from coloring books; or Zach, the raver/gamer I was "in love with."

My crush on Zach was a rebellion against myself. I knew he wasn't cute or cool or funny, didn't have any hobbies I related to, didn't seem sweet or nice, and never said anything interesting. But the lack of substance to my crush only fueled my interest in him. *Logic doesn't have any role in love,* I thought. *This funny feeling in my heart, which feels both very good and very bad, is the only metric of love I'm concerned with.*

I sat between Zach and Tyler in English, and they would lean over my desk to make fun of each other, which, being a sad virgin for whom physical proximity to boys was the only known pleasure, I really enjoyed.

"Where'd you get those pants?" Tyler said, a sarcastic jab at Zach's giant swishy parachute pants bungeed at the ankle.

"PacSun," Zach said dryly. The pants were clearly not from PacSun.

"Fuck you, dude," Tyler said. The teacher heard this and sent Tyler to sit in the closet, a common punishment from this particular teacher.

Without Tyler around, my attempt at conversations with Zach seemed stilted.

"Tyler is so weird," I said.

"I hate that guy," Zach said.

I loved how angry and sarcastic Zach was. I loved that he hated things so openly. I wanted to hate things too, instead of feeling the detached resentment I felt about most things. I wanted to feel passionate about something. I wanted to hate Tyler if only to have something in common with Zach. But Tyler was a necessary lubricant in my conversations with Zach, and I liked him for that reason. Also he was funny and easy to talk to and had a cute center part and smelled a little like warm bread.

"I hate him too," I said.

I had touched Zach's penis once, on a road near a river. We were both very drunk, and he asked me to touch it, so I did. I had cupped and petted the flaccid thing for close to a minute, unsure of what was supposed to happen. My wrist was getting tired from being pressed against his stomach underneath the still-buckled silver studded belt that held up his gigantic denim parachute pants as we stood in the middle of a mostly unused dirt road a few yards away from our friends. *Should I squeeze it?* I thought. *Should I milk it?*

"What should I do?" I said.

"Never mind," he said. "You're drunk."

It was a relief to let go.

One night, at Marcy's house, Marcy tricked me into eating a significant portion of a pot brownie by telling me that it was a regular brownie that she had made herself and that it would hurt her feelings if I didn't at least taste it. After I ate it, she disappeared into another room to argue with her boyfriend on the phone. I wrapped myself up in a blanket and breathed deeply in and out, convinced I was experiencing a panic attack. Goth Ryan knocked on Marcy's door and when I answered it, he asked me to go outside. He wanted to talk about his feelings.

"Is this happening?" I said. "Are you here?"

"I like you so much," he said, initiating a hug. "I used to think about hurting myself all the time, but now whenever I start thinking about that, I think about you instead. I feel so much better lately. You are a wonder. I've never met anyone like you."

I started imagining that he was talking to me about raspberries. I imagined that he was trying to offload raspberries onto me because the raspberries weren't very good and he had to get rid of them. He had so many raspberries that he would have to devote the rest of his life to getting rid of them. I imagined Goth Ryan becoming the CEO of a raspberry-offloading company that marketed the raspberries to people by using slogans like "I like these raspberries so fucking much," and "The way I feel about these raspberries is so much better than the way I normally feel about raspberries," and "Buy these goddamn raspberries or I'll fucking kill myself." It was endearing to me that he thought he could sell raspberries using emotional manipulation. That kind of naïveté was sweet, in a way. In retrospect I see that I was super, super stoned.

"I'm going to try to get a job," he said. "I want to take care of you."

I nodded and rubbed my increasingly dry and puffy eyes,

simultaneously acutely aware of, frustrated with, and incapacitated by my role in the universe.

Something was weird about this. Ryan seemed to be saying he was in love with me, but I knew he was sleeping with my best friend, and seemed to not notice that I didn't love him back, even though I kind of did. So what was the problem? I couldn't remember what I was trying to think about. What was the question?

"I need to go inside and . . . ask Marcy . . . something . . . about . . . fruit," I managed to say.

"Okay, I'm going to take off, then," he said. He kissed me on my temple and held my hand as I moved away from him, and we maintained intense eye contact as I went inside and closed the door.

"Ryan is here?" Marcy said. "Where the fuck did he go?"

"Um," I said, "I feel really weird right now."

"You should just go out with him already. He is totally in love with you. He didn't even come in to say hi to me."

"I think I might be having a seizure."

"Oh, you poor thing!" she said with a big smile. "You ate too much pot brownie! Here, lie down, sweetie."

"Goddamnit, Marcy."

"Everybody has to grow up sometime," she said, still smiling.

"God, I fucking hate you."

Marcy and I quickly became inseparable frenemies. I didn't trust her with any kind of secret, and emotional support seemed to go one way (from me to her), but we were both weird and encouraged each other's weird behavior, and I enjoyed the fact that we didn't completely like each other. I didn't expect much from her, so she couldn't really disappoint me. And I didn't have to worry about hiding the unappealing parts of myself from her. More importantly, Marcy was my social crutch, and I was her scapegoat. She made all the plans, got boys to hang out with us, and found rides everywhere. And I would take the fall if anything happened so she wouldn't look bad in front of her grandma or boyfriend or people she had crushes on or whoever else she happened to be worried about impressing at any given time. She would say, "Sorry we were out so late, Grandma. Chelsea wanted to make out with Ryan all night," and her grandma would tell me that if I wanted to keep sleeping over I had to start going to church with them. Later, Marcy would tell me, "Don't worry, I'll make it up to you," and invite Zach over to drink Jägermeister and watch TV with us. I was being mobilized and crippled simultaneously, but I was fine with this setup.

Marcy invited Zach over one Saturday night, when her grandma would be visiting family. While we waited for Zach's dad to drop him off, Marcy called Goth Ryan and invited him to join us.

"I'm not just going to sit there and watch you and Zach make out," she said.

Marcy selflessly swept Goth Ryan away to her room as soon as he arrived. Before he disappeared, I tried to give him a look that said *I don't care what you do*, and *Like, at all*, and *Anyway Zach is here and we are in love, we are going to tell each other how in love we are and soon you will be merely a distant foggy memory that rarely occurs to me, and when I'm older I will conflate you with someone else I knew around this time and you will become a half-person, so unimportant on your own that I couldn't even be bothered to remember you as one being, so utterly useless in my memory that you barely exist*, and *But in all seriousness, I really don't care.*

Zach and I watched *The Simpsons*, filled up on Jäger, and pretended not to hear the occasional moaning and knocking coming from Marcy's room. We slowly became drunker and more sideways, until we were lying cheek-to-cheek on the couch, both facing the TV.

"You think that's funny?" Zach whispered, feeling my smile

against his face, a reaction to something Lisa Simpson said about Disney California Adventure.

"Yeah," I said, pretending to be short of breath for some reason.

"You're wonderful," he said.

I smiled again, somewhat suspicious of the similarity of this declaration to Ryan's description of me as "a wonder." I imagined that Marcy was secretly choreographing my entire love life, choosing the people I would have my first sexual experiences with, telling them what to say. Maybe she was working her way toward some massive humiliating punch line that more or less plagiarized the movie *She's All That*. Something like: "Oh, you thought you were actually cool? Oh, you thought people would like you without me telling them to?"

"Stay right there," he said, getting up and moving the coffee table away from the couch. "Now hang your head over the edge. I want to kiss you upside down."

Zach and I kissed a little and then continued watching TV. I tried to dismiss my paranoid thoughts about Marcy. I tried to tell myself that she had control over my social life because I was unable to coordinate one for myself, not because she was some kind of mastermind scheming to fuck me over. Zach had kissed me because he liked me and was attracted to me. He had called me wonderful because he saw that I was different from everybody else, different from Marcy, and was amazed by the wonder that I was. I had to learn to accept the good things that came my way, instead of overanalyzing them until they disappeared.

"I like you, Zach," I said.

"I like you, too."

The next Sunday before church began, Marcy and I whispered to each other about the other people arriving to church.

"Can you believe the world's greatest lover is here?" I said, gesturing to an unshaved, dehydrated-looking man with an oversize white

T-shirt that read WORLD'S GREATEST LOVER in a cartoon font on both the front and the back.

"Oh my god, we're so close. We have to try to talk to him," Marcy said.

"We should give him some privacy. I'm sure he gets harassed by girls like us all the time."

"I'm pretty sure he wants the attention if he's wearing a giant fucking T-shirt advertising his talents."

The world's greatest lover stood up to make an announcement about the need for volunteers for the upcoming potluck, and we both lost it.

"Be respectful," Marcy's grandma said to Marcy.

"Why don't you tell Chelsea?" Marcy said.

The tic in my butt started acting up after the sermon started, as sometimes happened when I was in a confined space or forced to be still. I was sitting right next to Marcy, and I knew she could feel it. I had told her about my tics, but I had never been right next to someone while it happened. I was embarrassed, but scooting over would only transfer my mortifying butt motion onto some stranger. My butt tic increased in speed due to the stress.

"It's all right," Marcy whispered to me. "You're okay."

On Monday, Marcy found me in the school courtyard to tell me that Zach had given her a letter that morning explaining that he was in love with her. She told me she felt sad for Zach, and guilty that she had to let him down.

"I mean, I have a boyfriend," she said.

I didn't ask to see the letter, for fear of exposing the pride that made me doubt, at least partially, the existence of such a letter.

"I'm sorry," she said. "I know how much you like him."

"It's not your fault," I said. I had never hated a girl as much as I did in that moment.

Later in English class, Tyler turned to me and whispered, "Wanna screw?" He held his hand out to me, revealing a single flat-head screw. It was dopey and perverted but there was something sweet about it. Normally I would have turned to Zach, made some kind of facial expression or gesture to indicate that Tyler lacked the intelligence and grace I desired in a partner. But I chose not to acknowledge Zach.

"Yeah," I said. I took the screw from Tyler and stuffed it into my pocket. "Thank you. I appreciate it."

I could see from a sideways glance that Zach was not looking at me.

After school, Marcy and I had a few hours to kill before Goth Ryan and Marcy's boyfriend could hang out with us, so we walked to Marcy's cousin's house down some dirt road a couple miles away from the main part of town. This was a part of town that I should have known the name of—I had spent nearly my whole life here, in and around Clearlake—but this was not the kind of information I tended to keep in my brain. I was allowing myself to be taken places with no actionable plan for how to get myself to a phone or a neighborhood that I could identify by name.

Marcy's cousin wasn't home. With nowhere else to go, we approached two adult men, one of whom was shirtless, drinking beer on a nearby porch.

"Hey, what's up?" Marcy said.

"Just drinking beers, too hot to do much," the shirtless man said. "You're welcome to join us."

We entered the house and used their phone to call Marcy's boyfriend and Goth Ryan, to tell them to meet us at this stranger's house.

I briefly wondered if Zach lived in the neighborhood. I didn't know where he lived, so every place I went seemed like an opportunity to run into him.

The house was hot and stale. There were seven or eight men sitting around a dining table, cigarettes burning in each person's hand, beer cans scattered everywhere. Marcy and I got drunk very quickly from a bottle of vodka that was being passed around. We played some kind of drinking card game with the men. They stared at us, and Marcy and I teased and flirted with each other, knowing how cute we must look in their eyes, what a spectacle we were. We hugged and rested our heads on each other's shoulders and forced shots down each other's throats. We took shots between turns, on other people's turns, and from the floor well after the game was over. We stumbled into the backyard, where I steadied myself on a garbage can and looked into the sky for celestial clues about where I was.

It started getting dark, and Goth Ryan and Marcy's boyfriend still hadn't shown up. We didn't have a plan for getting home, and we were way too drunk to start planning something, or even to coherently discuss what we might do if the guys didn't show up.

If you had to choose, I thought, drunkenly forgetting the issue at hand and replacing it with semilyrical melodrama, *is it better to be with someone who you love or who loves you?*

I wish I could tell you I had some deep emotional scarring or perverse desire for pain that caused me to act this reckless. I wish, even, that I could tell you that I was just a stupid fifteen-year-old who didn't see the problem with getting raging drunk in a strange house with a bunch of adult men whom I had never met before, with a girl considerably more reckless than I was. But I wasn't stupid. I knew what could happen to me and I just didn't seem to give a shit.

"Ryan has a Prince Albert," Marcy whispered into my ear, hugging me from behind.

"What does that mean?" I said. I tried to nudge her away from me. I didn't feel like flirting with her anymore.

"A dick piercing. It's hot."

"Okay. Very cool," I said.

Marcy kissed my neck and I suddenly became aware that—surrounded by strange men who all looked the same to me, none of whom had given us their names, at 1 a.m., in a part of town I probably couldn't find on a map—maybe I actually did give a shit about what happened to me.

"Please don't kiss me," I whispered, not wanting to embarrass her—not because I was a nice person but because I was afraid of her retaliation. Then, drunkenly realizing that I shouldn't have to tiptoe around her just to avoid one of her vindictive tirades, I said more loudly, "Get off of me," and scrunched my shoulders to make hugging me more difficult.

Marcy and I would only hang out like this for a couple more months. We were already becoming sick of each other's shit, and sick of the workarounds we had developed to minimize having to deal with each other's shit, and sick of seeing who we would pretend to be in order to appease each other. I was sick, for example, of trying to make myself appear emotional when she was crying just so she would trust me enough to tell me why she was crying, which was often for a reason I found disappointing. And I was sick of maintaining a consistent level of shyness to avoid upstaging her.

"You're such a fucking bitch," she said. "You're such a fucking pussy little bitch. Hit me. I know you want to, you fucking stupid bitch."

"Shut up," I said. I had some real zingers back then.

"Just hit me, you stupid slut. I want you to. I won't hit you back. I want you to hit me, you fucking stupid pussy."

She was making it sound pretty good. I slapped her on the cheek.

"You fucking bitch, I can't believe you did that," she said, and slapped me back.

Blood started pouring from my nose onto my clothes and the carpet we were standing on. To be fair, she hadn't hit me that hard. I've always been prone to nosebleeds.

"You need to call your mom," Marcy said almost immediately, as a joke I guessed, but who could really tell with her?

I pinched my nose hard, walked to the bathroom, and stuck

my face under the sink faucet. I knew there were certain things you could do to make a bloody nose stop bleeding, but I didn't do any of them. I just let water run over my nose, washing some of the blood down the drain but mostly just diluting it and splashing it all over my face and the sink.

"Chelsea," a male voice said, entering the bathroom. I imagined that Zach had seen me and Marcy fighting in the backyard somehow. Maybe he lived around here after all. Maybe he had come to rescue me, to explain that the note he'd given to Marcy had been misinterpreted, or that she had made it up, to tell me again that I was wonderful. We would walk off into the sunset and I would touch his penis, miraculously knowing what to do this time, and he would like it.

I could hear the familiar din of Marcy fighting with her boyfriend somewhere else in the house.

"I'm sorry we're so late," the voice said. I was being hugged from behind by pale, claw-like hands with black fingernail polish wrapping around my waist.

"It's okay," I said, and intentionally blew out the blood clot that was beginning to slow the flow of my bloody nose. I wanted my nose to keep bleeding. I wanted Goth Ryan to see what I let Marcy do.

I watched the blood drip onto the ceramic sink, splattering into dozens of tinier droplets and then recollecting to form lines that emptied into the drain. I considered stopping the drain so I could see how much blood I was losing.

"I want you to be my girlfriend," he said, making no indication of whether he approved or disapproved of the blood pouring out of my skull.

I looked up at myself in the mirror. Goth Ryan was still holding my waist. I made a face at my reflection that I had seen cartoon characters make to indicate a resignation to something unpleasant but inevitable: eyelids half closed, making direct eye contact with the camera, lips pursed.

"Yeah, great," I said, still looking at my reflection. "That would be perfect."

But my sarcasm sounded false and cloying. I knew I wasn't the victim I wanted to believe I was. I knew that I was letting my nose continue to bleed. I was not making any effort to stop it.

8

CERAMIC BUSTS

"Hey," I said. He didn't hear me.

I was shy enough to have waited until the fourth day of driving school to say something to him, but not so shy that I wouldn't insert myself into company that didn't explicitly want me. I was selectively shy. Or I wasn't shy at all, but awkward and antisocial. Anyway, in this case, I had nothing to lose. This driver's ed course was only two weeks long, and I was only in Los Angeles visiting my dad for three weeks. He looked like the star of a movie about cool teenagers. His scarf and denim jacket were extremely impractical for the Los Angeles summer. His long mousy hair covered most of his face, so mostly what I was attracted to, I guess, was the exposed tip of his nose and his mouth and chin.

The class was mostly made up of adults who had been court-mandated to complete a driver's training course after what I presumed was negligent driving. There was one other nerdy teenage girl who was trying to get her learner's permit, like me and this boy.

"Hey," I said again, sitting down next to him on a bench during a class break. "I'm Chelsea."

"Sandy," he said.

I said nothing else, confident about where the conversation had gone.

It was as if my whole life to this point had just been practice, and this was the real thing. The perfect boy. The limited time frame. The rigid, semi-educational setting.

Sandy stood up and took a call on his cell phone. He walked to the street and kicked the fence halfheartedly with his white Converse. I watched him unapologetically, knowing immediately that I was in love.

I was really good at and experienced with being in love. I can't remember a time in my teenage or even childhood years when I wasn't hopelessly and obsessively in love with someone. It was just how I operated. The moment before I met Sandy, I was in love with Zach the angry raver, and before him a guy named Sage who I had briefly met and never really talked to, and before him Jake, who was technically my boyfriend but who I also never talked to, and before him a more positive raver whose screen name was CapricornBoi78 and who was three years older than I was and also gay, and before him a boy in my ceramics class who I made no effort to get to know and who I called Purple Shirt Boy, and that was just in the previous eighteen months.

"Cool scarf," I said the next day during our lunch break. "Kinda warm, though."

"I like the way winter clothes look. I wish it were winter all year long."

"Yeah, it looks cool," I said.

Sandy stood up and walked over to the bathroom. I waited on the bench. A few minutes later he exited the bathrooms and walked away from the driving school, onto the sidewalk, and out of sight.

The next day I wore my Beck T-shirt and red polyester plaid bell-bottoms and square-toed green plaid low-tops. This was my best outfit.

"Do you like Beck?" I said during our class break, the only ten minutes I would have with him all day.

"Beck's cool," Sandy said.

"I'm going to see his concert this weekend."

"Cool."

"Beck is my favorite musician."

"That's cool."

"Who do you like?"

"I don't know. I've been listening to Rooney lately. They're my friends, though, so it kinda doesn't count."

"Oh, I haven't heard of them. I'll check it out."

"Yeah, their singer is the brother of the drummer from Phantom Planet."

"Oh, I love Phantom Planet," I said.

"Yeah."

I knew for sure that I would make Sandy my boyfriend. Despite his disinterest, despite our limited time frame, despite the huge disparity between our levels of coolness, I was going to get this boy to love me. I would go back to Clearlake and become much closer to the friends I had so I could tell them about my long-distance L.A. boyfriend, Sandy, who would sound exotic and foreign to their small-town ears. I would tell them he hung out with Rooney, a band that my friends would not know about but would still find impressive.

"Rooney is the band of the brother of one of the guys from Phantom Planet," I would say patiently, and my friends would still not know what I was talking about because they would not be as worldly as I was.

"Which planet?" they would say.

"Music. Hello?" I would say.

Most likely, my friends would be "friends" in the loosest sense of the word. I wouldn't be able to talk to them about the little fights I had with Sandy over the phone late on school nights. Or, I could talk to them about it, but they wouldn't be able to respond with emotional depth or related personal anecdotes the way I would want them to, as that would be what I would have become accustomed to by talking to

Sandy. And so, over time, I would stop telling my "friends" anything about my inner life and save it all for phone dates with Sandy, who would become my best and only friend. Probably I would accidentally reveal this to him one night when I was feeling particularly vulnerable and he would silently freak out about my dependence on him, and it would cause just enough of a rift between us for him to be seduced by some cool, chill girl who also hung out with Rooney and who had many friends whom she could burden with her emotional crises, if she ever even had any. And suddenly our phone dates would end and all I would have were my "friends," who would be starting not to like me because of how distant and condescending I had been while dating Sandy, and I would have to find ways to win them over again, like maybe by becoming a good listener or a generous compliment giver.

"My favorite Beck song is 'Thunder Peel,'" I said. "The one that's like, *Now I'm rolling in sweat with a loaf of cold bread and a taco in my jeans.*"

I had practiced singing the lyrics over the weekend, perfecting my falsetto delivery. I'd hoped that it would make him smile.

"Oh," Sandy said.

I giggled.

The Monday after the Beck concert I brought my digital camera to driving school and showed Sandy the pictures I had taken at the show. I described the nosebleed seats my dad had bought for my cousin and me, and how we had snuck into the area by the stage so I could take better photos. My cousin had been detained by a security guard, but I'd gone ahead without her.

"I was molested in the mosh pit," I told him. "But it was still worth it."

The photos were crisp and vivid, with highly saturated pink and cyan backgrounds, a lot like the photos in the *Midnite Vultures* CD insert.

"Do you like that album?" I said.

"Sure."

Sandy got up and walked away from me, and I turned the camera to film mode and collected a few seconds of footage of him walking across the parking lot, idling in the middle of the courtyard to look at his phone, then walking away again as he lifted the phone to his ear. The next day I got a few more seconds as I pretended to look through the photos on my camera while walking toward him.

"I'm gonna go get some gum," Sandy said. "Do you want to come?"

He led me to the crosswalk and then to a liquor store across the street. I followed him down the narrow aisles, then to the cash register, and then back out to the street. He gestured to me that he wanted to jaywalk. I hesitated. I didn't have anything against jaywalking per se, but it wasn't really my personal style.

"Come," he said gently.

I jaywalked. I jaywalked with him and decided that every time I jaywalked in the future I would dedicate the act to Sandy, which I didn't mean literally but which I can't help thinking about every time I jaywalk, even now.

We went back to class. The next day we started behind-the-wheel driving with individual instructors, and I never saw Sandy again.

On my computer I zoomed in on a particularly good video still of Sandy. He was smiling slightly, his head turned toward me, presumably looking at me but with his eyes completely covered by his hair. The collar of his denim jacket was slightly askew, which added, I felt, a degree of vulnerability.

I drew this image just as I saw it, in graphite on a piece of printer paper. I filled in the bulk of his hair with the edge of my pencil, and used the tip on the finer detail work around his mouth and jawline and the edge of his face. I made up lines where the digital image was pixilated or unclear. I hung the drawing on my bedroom wall. It was better than the images on my computer, even if it was less precise and the perspective was off, because its strokes were made by my hand. The hours that were lost making it were hours from my life. It was almost as if I had touched him, this boy who was irretrievably gone from my life. It was almost like I could still touch him.

I made a second, quicker drawing and took it to school with me. I made a ten-inch bust in ceramics class based on the second drawing. I glazed it with bright blue and forest green, and white for his pale, hair-covered face.

I understood that I was being creepy. That I had just been overcome by meeting someone who was not from Clearlake, who had none of the baggage or the simplicity that came with being from Clearlake. I knew I should be embarrassed to be making a ten-inch ceramic bust of someone I had known for ten days and who had shown very little interest in me. Still, somehow, especially now that he was definitively out of my life forever, I felt like he was mine.

I had finished most of my high school requirements by junior year, so in senior year I had time to take five elective classes each semester. I could have taken AP classes for college credit, but instead I opted to have my ceramics teacher create a new class title for each of my elective periods so that I could stay in the ceramics studio all day while still technically being in different classes.

I wasn't actually that into ceramics as a medium. I didn't feel there was any particular reason to create something three-dimensional. But I loved my ceramics electives because for once I felt ambitious and inspired, eager to improve my skill set, and increasingly confident about my artistic ability.

I made a second, smaller ceramic bust. I made a 24-by-36-inch painting using bright pink, green, and cyan, inspired by the *Midnite Vultures* CD insert that I had mentioned to Sandy. My ceramics teacher asked me if I wanted to learn screenprinting as an after-school project and I said that I did, and I made a four-color print of Sandy, edition of fifty.

"Who is that?" my friend James asked me, after seeing dozens of depictions of the same dude.

"Somebody I met in driving school," I said.

"He looks really cool."

I felt impressed by my own lack of shame, my obsessiveness, my insatiable desire to keep Sandy in my life through art. I was spending hours and hours of class time, and hours and hours of free time, making portraits of someone with whom I'd had *nothing*. The art was, in fact, making any future relationship with Sandy impossible. Even if he were to magically appear before me again, or if I were able to find him on Myspace, the art I had made of him was too much, too crazy, my feelings too out of touch with reality. I could never explain that I had made fifteen portraits of him in at least five mediums over the course of eight months.

It was horribly pathetic, and yet I didn't care. Actually, I liked the fact that I might appear pathetic through my art. Or I liked that I had deliberately chosen to make myself appear that way, instead of it happening on its own without my specific approval, as it had in the past.

My obsession became more interesting to me than the content of my work, which is to say that I found myself interested in myself, which was new and exciting. I liked that I was becoming the kind of person who would prioritize art making over protecting my own image as a nonpsychotic person.

I was embracing parts of myself that I normally tried to keep hidden. I felt in control of my flaws in a way that made me like my flaws.

And I was fascinated that a visual representation of someone I found visually appealing could be interesting conceptually, though I also liked the portraits visually. I was amazed that my feelings of loneliness and self-loathing and unrequited desire could be used to create something that I liked, wanted to be around, and wanted to show other people.

I applied to art school the next year, and I submitted my collected portraits of Sandy as my portfolio.

9

A SCRAP OF HELLO KITTY NOTEPAPER

In junior year of high school I became the bassist in a metal parody band called Sparkling Honeypuff. But if you asked my bandmates, Brandon and Charlie, they would probably have told you we were in a serious thrash metal band called Slaughtered Goat (or something), and they would probably have made some mean joke about how I couldn't play even the simplest bass chords despite their six-plus months of effort to teach me. To this I would have said that it was funnier overall if I didn't really know how to play bass, more in line with the parody aspect of the band, and also that it was more fun to simply hang out and have a good time than to listen to the same Black Sabbath song over and over, and slide my fingers across rough strings that gave me blisters, trying to imitate the bass line of some song I didn't even like.

"How can you not like Black Sabbath?" Brandon would say.

"Is that a real question?" I would say, completely mystified. "You honestly like this music?"

These kinds of creative differences ultimately led to the band's demise, at which point Brandon and Charlie started a new band, also called Slaughtered Goat (or whatever) with a new bassist, a role they didn't actually fill.

I had known I wasn't a musician since my second-grade keyboard recital, during which I stopped playing in the middle of the song and yelled to the audience, "I don't know the rest!" I liked the idea of being part of a group and contributing to something larger than myself, and hanging out with my friends under the guise of being productive, but I didn't actually want to play music. Especially not metal.

"Can I be the bassist in your new band?" I asked Charlie.

"Um," said Charlie. "I'll have to ask Brandon. We might not need a bassist."

"Brandon is right there. Why don't you ask him now?"

They let me back into the band after a small degree of persistence and manipulation, but things were never the same. For one, I had to promise never to refer to the band as Sparkling Honeypuff; also, we never had band practice again. Or, at least, I was never invited to band practice again.

"We're never going to get the gig if we don't work together on some jams," I said to Charlie.

"What are you even talking about?" he said.

When I was invited to be the photographer for my friend Logan's metal band, Broken Femur, I eagerly accepted. I didn't like the responsibility of being in a band anyway; being a photographer was more my speed. I went to all of their practices and house shows, where I would halfheartedly snap a few action shots with my digital camera and then spend the rest of the night looking for snacks. Later, I would upload the photos onto my computer and never look at them or do anything with them again. It was a pretty sweet gig.

I first saw Sage at a Battle of the Bands concert that Broken Femur was competing in, which took place on my high school football field one Saturday in the summer.

"Who is that?" I said, looking at a pale, skinny dude with black bell-bottoms, no shirt, and shiny brown hair down to his butt.

"Which one? Tony?" Logan said. "Oh, that one? Sage. He's the drummer in Johnny's band."

Maybe a hippie boy version of Alanis Morissette isn't everyone's idea of the perfect man, but it was mine. I took a few photographs of him with my camera, then switched to video mode and filmed a five-second clip of him walking across the field.

I didn't see Sage again until Logan had a New Year's Eve party six months later in the trailer adjacent to his parents' house. I recognized Sage immediately, most likely due to how many times I had watched the clip I'd filmed the summer before. He wore the same bell-bottoms low on his waist, and I could see he was not wearing underwear. I ignored him for hours while trying to get as drunk as possible and playing Quarters with Brandon and Charlie.

Quarters is a game with simple rules: You put your knuckles on a table while your opponent launches quarters at your hand from the other side of the table. Every time they break the skin on your knuckles they get a point. It is probably a good way to contract blood-borne infectious diseases, and an even better way to physically hurt people who have kicked you out of a band you were inexplicably desperate to be in.

Eventually I was drunk enough that I had the confidence to poke Sage with a stray drumstick as he walked past me. He looked at me as if I was a drunken moron and disappeared into some other room.

I had kissed boys before. Plenty of them. I kept a single sheet of lined Hello Kitty paper tracking the names of everyone I'd kissed, and the paper was almost filled to capacity. There were boys I'd kissed while drunk. Boys I'd kissed while playing Truth or Dare when I was eleven. (It counted.) Boys I'd kissed while they were drunk and I was pretending to be drunk. Boys I'd heard from reliable sources that I'd kissed but couldn't remember kissing because I had been too drunk. I looked at the list periodically to reassure myself that I was someone worth kissing. I wasn't exactly anxious to add more names to the list, but I knew that if I wrote the next name big enough, the next name after that name would have to go on the other side of the paper, or another piece of paper altogether. At that point I could even begin to refine the taxonomy. But mostly I wanted a boyfriend. It was the middle of my senior year and I had never really had one.

It seemed miraculous that anyone ever accomplished the task of finding someone they were willing to admit they liked who happened to like them back. When I liked someone I tended to stay far away from that person until my desperation became overwhelming, and I would force myself to approach them with no plan of what to say. Then, standing in front of them, I would have to think of something to say on the spot, such as "Can I have a pen? I can't give it back, though. It's complicated."

"I don't," the person would say, gesturing to the soccer field that surrounded us, on which our classmates apathetically kicked a ball around.

"Oh, that's cool," I would say, smiling and rolling my eyes, trying to convey that I was a chill girl with no pressing need for a pen.

Toward the end of the night, a guy I had seen hanging out with Sage most of the night approached me. He was drunk.

"What's your name?" he said.

"Chelsea," I said. "What's yours?"

"I'm Brian. What are you doing after the party?" He was pale, and had long, tangled dark hair like a rag doll. He seemed drugged out, stumbling while attempting to stand in one spot. I didn't usually appreciate the drugged-out look, but it was a good look on him. He looked like a careless trashy rock star in need of heroin.

"I don't know." It was well past midnight, and I wasn't planning on doing anything else. "I'm supposed to call my mom if I can't find a ride home."

"I can give you a ride home. I'm going to my sister Hannah's house for an after-party but I can give you a ride in a little while."

"How many people are going?" I said.

"Just me, Hannah and her boyfriend, Dave, that guy over there, Sage, and maybe our buddy Richard."

I made some quick drunken calculations. If I left with Brian there was a good chance I would not make it home. Unfulfilled drunken promises of rides home were common in my life. I did not know any of these people and I wasn't sure if any of my friends knew them, there was always the possibility of rape, and my friends might be mad at me for leaving. But Sage was going to be there.

I told Logan I was leaving with Brian and his friends, and Logan gave me a concerned, almost fatherly look. He never drank and so was often forced to be the voice of reason for his alcoholic friends.

Charlie fell or was pushed into the kitchen counter behind Logan, breaking the counter and causing the sink to fall into the cabinet below. People laughed and *oooh*ed as Charlie tried to pick himself up out of the broken sink. Still, Logan seemed more concerned with my safety than with the damage to his property.

"You can stay here if you want, you know," he said.

"It's okay. They said they'd give me a ride home."

"What do you like to do for fun, Chelsea?" Brian said.

"I like to paint," I said, trying to see Sage's reaction in my periphery. "And, um, photography." Then, completely forgetting the question, I added, "I go to high school."

"How old are you?" A joint was being passed around but I declined to participate, as I had decided to "never smoke pot" a few years earlier.

"Seventeen."

"Sweet," said Brian. He put a hand on my shoulder and smiled at me.

"How old are you?" I said.

"Twenty-one."

"Your fly is down," I said to Sage, forgetting to look at him briefly before I said it, as I had planned, so that it wouldn't be obvious that I had seen that it was down hours earlier and had intentionally delayed giving him the information so that it could continue to be a conversation-starting option, and so that it seemed that for most of the night I hadn't bothered to look at his crotch.

He wordlessly zipped it up and smiled at me.

"I'll need to go home soon," I said to Brian, knowing already that I was not going to be driven home.

"I can't drive you home. I'm too drunk," said Brian. It was 2 a.m. I called my mom and told her in my best attempt at sounding sober that I was spending the night at my new friend Hannah's house, and gave her the address where she could pick me up in the morning. I was becoming increasingly worried about the sleeping arrangements, and of the intentions and/or tenacity of Brian, who had probably never meant to drive me home. I sat between them on the couch, wishing Logan was there to tell me what to do.

"I'm really tired," said Sage.

"Me too," I said.

"You can sleep on the couch," Brian said. "Sage and I will sleep on the floor."

"No way," Sage said. "This is my couch. Chelsea can share with me if she wants, though."

I wish I could say that I usually had more grace and subtlety than my actions at this point suggest, but the truth was I did not surprise myself by leaping onto Sage and beginning to kiss his neck and face. Brian scooted off the couch and onto the floor.

In the morning, Sage had large red hickeys covering his neck. I had never given anyone a hickey before, and I was astonished by how easy it had been. I didn't even remember doing it. Sage pulled his long hair into a bun, exposing his entire neck, evidently unashamed of the damage I'd done.

"It looks like you were stuck in a cage all night with a rabid monkey," Hannah said.

Sage laughed. "It was worth it," he said.

I checked my own neck in the bathroom and noticed one small tender mark, which I covered up with some of Hannah's makeup so that my mom wouldn't see it when she picked me up.

At home, I unfolded my sheet of Hello Kitty paper and wrote Sage's name at the bottom, filling what remained of the page.

On Monday at school, I recounted the details of this most exciting make-out session to friends, who mostly didn't care.

"Oh, that guy?" Logan said. "That's weird."

"I'm in love with Sage," I said, feigning melodrama by covering my heart with my right hand to conceal the very real melodrama I was feeling.

Sage was possibly the hottest guy I had ever seen in person. I had fantasized about him for six months, thinking I would never see him again, and then I'd kissed him. It was surreal. It felt like a teen movie, the kind where the protagonist loses her virginity at the end and everyone rejoices. I was that protagonist. This was my movie.

I was more eager than ever to participate in band-related events with Logan, as I thought it was my best chance at seeing Sage, who had my phone number but had not yet called. But Logan's band was taking some kind of hiatus.

"We're kind of just into writing and practicing right now," Logan said. "I don't think we're going to play any more shows this month."

"You're never going to get anywhere with that kind of attitude, you know," I said.

A few weeks later, I found myself at Hannah's house again. It turned out Sage was "without a home" and was sleeping on Hannah and Dave's couch in exchange for groceries purchased by Sage's mother. Sage had invited me over but had left soon after I arrived, as an awesome opportunity to practice drums with some members of his band had arisen, and that was not the kind of thing one can simply decline, apparently.

I did my best to react neutrally. I wanted to convey how great of a girlfriend I would be, if given the opportunity. I wouldn't be needy or inflexible. I could hang out with his friends while he casually ditched me.

I watched football with Hannah and Dave for hours and did my best to appear to believe I belonged there, which got easier as the day turned to night as Hannah and Dave made sure there was always a fresh beer in my hand. Brian arrived and appeared happy to see me, and I was happy to see someone who appeared happy to see me. He quoted some lyrics from the Darkness, which seemed ironic to me because I thought he looked like the singer from that band. I sang the rest of the line using my best chipmunk voice.

"*I believe in a thing called love / Just listen to the rhythm of my heart.*"

"Do you think the Darkness is a real band or a joke band?" Brian said. He had a slight Southern drawl for some reason, which made everything he said seem slightly sexual to me.

"What difference does it make?" I said.

"I just wonder if they take themselves super seriously or if they understand the irony."

"Definitely both," I said.

"Definitely?" he said, smiling, revealing his crooked, overcrowded teeth. "You sound pretty confident."

"I guess I could be wrong," I said, sitting on the arm of the couch and looking up at him, coming as close to flirtatious body language as I probably ever would.

Late in the night, when everyone was drunk, Sage came back to Hannah's house with his bandmates and intercepted my conversation with Brian to hug and kiss me. It felt more territorial than passionate, but I was delighted by it.

"She's a virgin," Dave said loudly to Sage. I suppose I knew, when they had asked me if I was a virgin earlier, that they would tell Sage. I suppose I wanted them to tell Sage, because I knew it made me special in a place like Clearlake, where nearly every girl lost her virginity by age thirteen, but I did find it a little odd that Dave chose to announce it the second Sage came home.

"Is that true?" Sage said, looking at me earnestly.

I declared my virginity to the whole room.

I had not held on to my virginity for any reason. It was incidental. It felt out of my control. And it didn't mean anything to me. I had simply never had the opportunity to get rid of it.

A few hours later, Sage asked me to be his girlfriend.

"Yes," I said very formally. "I will be that."

The next time we hung out, a couple of days later, Sage and I had sex. Hannah and Dave had made their bedroom available to us while they watched football in their living room with some friends.

Sage turned on a k.d. lang album and lit some incense. He was making an effort, I guess. I didn't really understand the appeal of k.d. lang but Sage was older and wiser and I had no experience with sex, so who was I to say what was sexy? I decided to keep an open mind about gross hippie music and stinky burning perfume sticks.

Sex was easy. Eerily easy. I checked several times to make sure that the right thing was happening down there, because I didn't feel much of anything. Wasn't it supposed to hurt? Wasn't I supposed to be crying and sopping up blood with my own underwear?

Sage reassured me several times that he had a big dick.

"There's no way for me to know if that's true or not," I said. But I sort of believed him, because how else would he have had the confidence to play k.d. lang, which I had determined was not sexy at all, not even a little bit, not even considering all the beers I had drunk at that point?

When we were done (when he was done), I felt extremely accomplished. Before I had even finished getting dressed, I started trying to figure out the right wording to use when I told my friends about my newfound state of womanhood. Basically it was a choice between "I lost my virginity" and "I had sex." I sort of hated the word "virgin," with its religious connotations or implications of sacredness, but saying "I had sex" seemed creepier and embarrassing. But that might be because I imagined saying it in a whisper, with the last word only mouthed and not spoken while making a creepy, villainous smile and widening my eyes as much as I could. So maybe if I said it in a normal tone of voice and didn't do anything weird with my face it wouldn't come off so creepy.

Sage and I left Hannah's bedroom and joined Hannah and Brian and the half-dozen people who I had been introduced to earlier but who still were nameless and random to me. I drank more beer and, for the first time, felt almost comfortable hanging out with this group of people, watching, for hours on end, a sport I could not begin to understand.

That night we slept on the couch, and I held on to Sage tightly, letting my hands fall to places they hadn't when we'd slept together before, places I had never explored on another human body. His butt, for example. He hugged me tightly and we breathed into each other's faces all night.

"I had sex," I said to Logan before class started on Monday, whispering the first two words and mouthing the last, my face scrunched up like a deranged and possibly rabid feral child.

"Really?" he said, trying to sound impressed by something that was not at all impressive. "Wow, cool!"

"It was cool," I said.

I started seeing Sage almost every weekend. My school was less than a block away from Hannah's house, so I would walk there after school on Friday, usually uninvited, and stay all weekend. Sage and I continued having sex. I didn't really understand what was so great about sex but I felt extremely excited by it nonetheless. It was strange and cool to be naked in front of another person, and strange and cool to see a naked person up close. In the moment, everything felt serious and straightforward. There was no pretense or humor or subtlety to any of our actions, just the flagrant search for pleasure—his, mostly. Afterward I felt embarrassed by how serious we had been, tried to make jokes about how weird naked bodies were, and then felt embarrassed about the jokes.

Sex, I would think happily to myself afterward. It was now a word that belonged to me. Everybody else in the world, and me.

Sometimes Sage would invite me to watch him practice with his band in the garage of a middle-aged developmentally disabled man who somehow had a lot of music equipment. Other times I would stay at Hannah's while Sage went to practice, and I would hang out with Brian.

"How's your painting going?' Brian said one day.

"What?" I said.

"You said you were a painter."

"Oh yeah. Good. Some of my paintings are on display in a meeting room for my school district, so that's pretty cool, I guess."

"You've got a lot of talent," he said.

"How would you know that? I've never shown you anything."

"I can sense these things, Chelsea," Brian said. "Oh, hey, do you want to go to my cousin's wedding?"

"Your cousin's wedding? Where is it?"

"Clearlake. Hannah and everybody will be there. I can pick you up."

"Is Sage going?"

"I think."

•

Sage seemed surprised to see me show up to the wedding of his roommate's cousin with his roommate's brother, but he didn't ask any questions. He hugged me and took my hand, leading me to a pew in the back of the church.

We held hands during the ceremony. He squeezed my hand at what felt like significant moments in the bride and groom's speeches, and I imagined his inner monologue describing all the great things about me, urging him to realize that I could be *this* for him, like in *The Little Mermaid* when Sebastian tries to get Prince Eric to kiss Ariel.

That night, we had sex on Hannah and Dave's couch after everyone had gone to sleep. Afterward, Sage calmly said, "I think we need to break up. I'm looking for a job right now and I know I'm not giving you the attention you deserve," and, without waiting for my response, gently fell into sleep.

I was too stunned to say anything, anyway. I stayed up for several hours, trying to figure out the best way to appreciate being wrapped in his arms while believing that I was likely never going to experience such a physical arrangement with anybody ever again.

In the morning, I said goodbye to Sage and waited in the driveway for my mom to pick me up.

At home, after crying for an hour in the shower, I found my scrap of Hello Kitty paper and threw it away. I didn't need it anymore. It was a relic of my childhood, which was gone now. I was a non-virgin woman who had "been with men," and who wasn't obsessed with the number of them she had been with, and who couldn't be bothered to remember their names.

And anyway, I had already transcribed the information into a Word document on my laptop and backed it up on an external flash drive.

10

SECRETS OF PROFESSIONAL TOURNAMENT POKER

My first conversation with my dad was short and strange.

Me: "Hello?"

My father: "How are you doing, sweetie?"

Me: "I'm fine. How are you?"

It was a telephone call I found myself on with no warning, and I wasn't sure yet what to think or feel. I made eye contact with my mom, who had handed me the phone after saying, "It's your dad, do you want to talk to him?" and then had stood there watching me as I reassessed everything that had happened in my life and everything I believed in.

My father: "I'm great."

He told me he had hired a private detective to find me, that the private detective had found my grandparents' phone number and address and given it to him, that my aunt had answered my grandparents' phone and given him our number.

He told me he was going to give my mom some money.

He told me he had been fishing recently, and asked for my mailing address. He wanted to send me a photo of the fish.

He said he set up a Hotmail account for me, which I could use to communicate with him.

I didn't know what to do with any of this information. I didn't know what it was supposed to mean. Something about the private detective troubled me. I was perplexed that he hadn't looked up our phone number himself in the phone book or online, or my grandparents' number for that matter, who still lived in the house my mom lived in when she and my dad were together. Hiring a private detective to get this information struck me as a very silly use of money.

I knew that my mom was seventeen when she became pregnant with me, and that my dad had been only fifteen. They'd met in detention a few months earlier. My dad had been scared and angry about my mom's decision to go through with the pregnancy and had disappeared from town. My mom told me about the intense loneliness and heartbreak she experienced throughout her pregnancy, but I'd always understood his decision to leave. Fifteen is too young to have a child, and too young to be held responsible for bad decisions. Similarly, my mom's decision to keep me in the face of all the very good reasons not to always struck me as strong-willed and impulsive. Both of my parents were stubbornly determined to live their lives the way they wanted to. It just so happened that only one of those life plans included taking care of me.

It was a brief conversation, and afterward we emailed each other once or twice a month. I logged on to the Hotmail account every couple of days with the sole purpose of seeing if he had sent me a message. I considered telling him that I already had multiple email accounts and didn't need another one, but I didn't want him to feel that I was insulted by his assumption that I didn't use email. Also, I thought maybe there was some higher logic to keeping our communication separated into its own email account. Maybe this was a fatherly decision that had nothing to do with how many email accounts I had. I didn't know how fathers thought.

I felt a little starstruck. When he did email me, I read his messages eagerly, marveling that he had any interest in talking to me. While in many ways he seemed like an average middle-aged man, he also seemed like a famous person, someone I always knew existed but never had access to before now.

I had two photographs of my dad when he was a teenager. I had found them in my mom's old photo albums when I was young, and kept them in a special keepsake box for years. He looked very different in each. One was an 8-by-10 photo that my mom developed in her photography class in high school of him and my mom, both smiling and blond, slightly washed out from the sunlight, both wearing dangly earrings and blazers. I could see parts of myself in him; the shape of my lips and the spacing between my teeth, the particular way my eyes squinted when I smiled. The other was a tiny school photo in which he looked sullen and dark and possibly Middle Eastern, and nothing like me at all. I could hardly understand how these photographs could be of the same person. Somehow the differences between the two photos made his existence seem surreal.

Two very different photos of the same person taken within a couple of years.

A person who I had believed without question would forever remain an enigma now emailing me at orange_chelsea_girl@hotmail.com. *Orange*, a color I would have said I hated if someone had asked me; *Chelsea*, the name my mom gave me because it sounded English and modern; *girl*, perhaps the only identifying detail my father knew about me.

In emails, he would tell me what was going on in his life and I would tell him about whatever my mom or brother was doing at the time, which seemed more interesting to me than whatever I was doing. He didn't ask me much about my life, and I didn't like talking about myself unless I was asked a question. Also, it wasn't obvious to me where our relationship was going: if this was supposed to be the beginning of a classic parent/daughter relationship, with heart-to-hearts and a reasonable amount of interest in all the boring details of each other's lives, like I had with my mom, or if this was just a conversation that would stop and start over the years with no real purpose, like the ones I had with some of my aunts and uncles. I didn't want to be caught making the wrong assumption.

I don't recall asking myself what my feelings were for him. I only recall the desperate search for signs indicating whether he loved me already or if that was something I was going to have to wait for.

I'd called my stepdad "Dad" once, when I was seven years old, right after his and my mom's wedding ceremony, and had been met with laughter. Seth and I hadn't really bonded, so it did feel a bit contrived for me to call him "Dad," but his laughter was shocking and upsetting, so I never used that word again.

When my mom became pregnant with my brother, River, a year later, I was thrilled. Not only had I always wanted a sibling, but I also thought a new baby would act as a glue to bind our tiny, mishmash family together. I was aware of myself trying extra hard to become close with Seth during my mom's pregnancy, when she became very sick and Seth was tasked with cooking for me and driving me to school. I asked him to play video games with me, to which he reluctantly obliged, told him I loved him in that cowardly way where I would run out the door before he had a chance to answer, and started using his last name, the one my mom took when she married him, the one my brother got when he was born, instead of my own, at school and in my diary, which I never pointed out to him and I doubt he ever knew.

As the excitement of the new baby wore off and the feeling of normalcy set in at home, it started to become clear to me that Seth saw me as *someone else's kid*. His opinion of me was much clearer now that I was able to compare his behavior toward me to his behavior toward River. He didn't love me the way he so obviously loved River. He had no interest in my interests, but had an intimate awareness of which objects River responded to in what ways at what time of day. He didn't hear me when I spoke unless I made a point of asking him a direct question, but was obsessed with trying to identify which words River was trying to say, impatiently waiting for his first word to be "Dada," though when River finally started talking, Seth and I were called the same thing, "Datties."

"She's using too much sour cream," Seth would say to my mom while we were all at the dinner table. I looked at him directly as he spoke about me, daring him to address me, but he didn't. "That shit is expensive. Tell her not to use so much."

"She likes sour cream," my mom would say. I would reach for another small scoop of sour cream and defiantly deposit it onto my baked potato, an early example of what would become my years-long dedication to making Seth as unhappy as possible in ways I could easily deny were intentional if I were ever questioned.

A few months after River was born, I developed a crippling fear of being away from my mom, even for an hour. I remember crying, *wailing*, at the threat of being taken to the county fair for the day with my beloved nana. It got so bad that I was even allowed to leave my third-grade class and go on home study for several months. I don't know exactly what I was afraid of, but I think it had something to do with the idea of the three of them—my mom, River, and Seth—being together, for even a minute, without me. The perfect, uncomplicated family unit, finally rid of the parasite child pathetically pretending to have the same last name.

Two years later, when my mom became pregnant with my sister, Kylie, I begged her to get an abortion, not because I didn't want another sibling, but because I couldn't bear the thought of my last name representing an even smaller fraction of the family than it already did. My mom considered the abortion (for totally different reasons, mostly having to do with her unstable relationship with Seth), but ultimately didn't go through with it. She gave Kylie both my last name and my brother's, connected by hyphen. It's still one of the most gracious things anyone has ever done for me.

•

After a year or so of emails, my dad told me he was going to come to Clearlake to meet me.

I felt angry at the thought of meeting him now. Anger was my go-to emotion at the time, but it seemed justified in this situation. Why now? Why had he waited a year? Why had he waited sixteen years? Why did he assume I wanted to meet him? Why did it feel like if I said no I would lose him again forever? Why was I suddenly considering him not being in my life a "loss" when I never had before?

I felt angry that he thought he had the right to enter my life whenever he found it most convenient, and I felt angry that he wanted to meet me at all, that he couldn't just commit to his decision to leave, that he selfishly put me in the position of having to meet the person who I had accepted would be irretrievably absent, who was now complicating the image I had of myself because now I had to be the daughter of another person and I didn't know how to do that. I had failed with my stepdad and I never expected to have to attempt something like that again, and I felt angry that he had such a lack of sensitivity that he would think it was appropriate not only to enter my life at all but also to enter my life when I was at an age that is known for being awkward and unbearable and confusing. I was sixteen, in a new high school, with new braces and a new prescription for birth control to alleviate my relatively new acne. In other words, I was feeling lonely, pathetic, ugly, vaguely horny, and desperate for bagels. (I was super into bagels.) Now I had this new issue to deal with, and no resources with which to work out my confusion.

"Why would you even consider not meeting him?" Marcy said.

"If you don't meet him, you'll always wonder," my ceramics teacher said.

"It's completely up to you," my mom said, determined to be neutral.

We planned to meet at his brother's house. Uncle Jett lived mere blocks from where we had lived for the past couple years, and only a few miles from everywhere we had lived before that. I wondered how many times my dad must have visited his brother there, and if he had known how close I had been to him at those times, or if he had thought about me at all before he decided to contact me. Maybe this was something he'd thought of spontaneously. Maybe he'd been looking through an old yearbook one day and thought, *Oh yeah, I got that girl pregnant. That daughter I have. I should see how that all shook out.* Or maybe he had thought about me a lot over the years. Maybe when he visited his brother he had looked us up in the phone book and drove past our house to see if we were home. Maybe he saw that we were home and panicked, drove to his brother's house, and talked it out with him.

My mom and I arrived at Jett's place and, amazingly, there was my dad, standing there, looking nothing like the two photos of him I had examined just that morning, extending his arms toward me.

My mom and my dad did most of the talking while I sat across from them quietly. *These are my parents*, I thought, feeling a vague appreciation for the history of the world, imagining all my ancestors sitting in the room with me and my parents, the whole of their lives culminating in the moment that was now occurring. Jett was in the kitchen adjacent to the living room making a mayonnaise-based guacamole that I would refuse to eat.

They talked about my teeth: how I had a couple that never came in and how it fucked up the orientation of the rest of my mouth, how braces had helped correct the orientation but how I still had to wear a partial denture until I got implants, which would need to happen someday, *hint, hint*. My dentist had told us that the issue was hereditary, and I could tell my mom was trying to get my dad to admit that he'd had his teeth fixed. He had clearly lost the gaps in his mouth that were visible in the smiling photo.

Then they talked about my acne: how they both had it pretty bad as teenagers but how mine seemed to be much, much worse, as if I had both of their worst breakouts ever on my face at once.

"It just doesn't seem to be going away," my mom said.

"She needs to use a benzoyl peroxide wash in the morning and a serum at night," he said.

"Yeah, we've tried all that," said my mom. "Birth control cleared up some of it, but the rest is pretty stubborn."

"She may need colon hydrotherapy at some point."

Meetings between parents and their estranged children looked so emotional and dramatic on TV. I had readied myself to be hugged and cried upon, and to be told in countless different ways that I was special and beautiful and that he was sorry he would never get to know the littler versions of me that were undoubtedly special and beautiful in their own ways.

When the five-year plan for tackling my acne had been settled, my parents and Jett began laughing and reminiscing about high school. There was no crying. I don't remember being hugged. I do remember thinking, *Fuck Carl Anders*, as they talked about someone none of them had seen since tenth grade.

Jett served snacks and gave us a tour of his house, and then my mom drove us the half-mile home.

I didn't hear from my dad again until months later, when he invited me on a trip to Mexico during spring break, with him, his girlfriend, Rozanna, and Jett's two children, Jessica and Aaron, who were twelve and thirteen and who I had never met.

We stayed at a luxury resort in Cabo San Lucas. Before then, the only hotels I'd ever stayed at were the cheap motels next to interstate freeways that my nana and papa rented when we went to Oregon to visit my cousins. We would spend the whole day at the motel, swimming in the outdoor pool and making up pool games, only leaving to eat at a local chain diner for dinner.

In Mexico, we had Mexican street food several times a day, ate fancy Italian dinners, toured the coast in a rented Jeep, listened to my dad carry on long conversations with locals in broken Spanish, and bought souvenirs from tourist shops.

There were no getting-to-know-each-other moments with my dad. There was no heart-to-heart about how weird it must be to suddenly have a second parent after spending your whole life believing you were never going to experience such a thing, or even about how weird it must be to suddenly have a teenage child after being a childless adult for many years. I didn't have any one-on-one time with him and there was no special treatment given to me over my cousins, who, judging from all the cute little nicknames they had for one another, had clearly spent time with him before. The idea that a man would be more interested in his own offspring than the offspring of others, as I had believed was the case with Seth, seemed not to apply in this situation.

I did feel drawn to Rozanna. She was beautiful and graceful and seemed able to remain detached from the emotional trajectories of the people around her and to enjoy her time in Cabo San Lucas as if it were a Mexican vacation, which I guess it was. What a strange woman, I thought, to go on vacation with her boyfriend's till-then estranged teenage daughter and her boyfriend's brother's children, without getting caught up in the complicated inner workings of that and enjoying full days on the beach with a magazine, never looking up. What a strange, amazing woman. I was hesitant to talk to her, not sure what I wanted to talk to her about, not wanting to insult my dad.

I blamed myself for the lack of conversation between me and my dad. I was too awkward, and too old to be so awkward, and I was too shy, and being shy was so stupid and embarrassing. I hated myself deeply and vividly, and was angry that I had allowed myself to believe that anyone else might feel any differently about me. I didn't blame my dad for not wanting to talk to me. I wouldn't want to talk to me either. I would want to be far away from me.

"Yum," I finally said the second day of our trip, somewhat desperately, referring to the Caprese salad, to the table of strangers that was supposedly my family, and was, unsurprisingly, ignored.

I wanted to make more of an effort. I wanted to be able to go home confident that I had done what was in my power to bond with these people.

"I love cilantro," I said quietly, meaning to say that I loved basil. I didn't bother to correct myself, and no one seemed to hear me anyway.

For the rest of the trip, I spoke only when someone asked me a direct question or when I had to order food. I retreated inward, berated myself for retreating inward, tried to be okay with being a person who retreated inward in an attempt to alleviate the anxiety that berating myself had caused, felt myself disconnecting from the group due to my endless emotional processing, and tried to be okay with being a person who disconnected from groups due to endless emotional processing.

I knew it was stupid, but I remember telling myself that I loved myself, and I remember it really helping.

At the end of the trip, my dad asked me to walk to the resort lobby with him to settle the bill. It was the only time we had alone together during the trip. On the way there, he said sharply, "There's no point in punishing me. The past is behind us."

"I'm not upset about the past," I said, excited to finally be addressing our relationship, the one thing I had prepared myself to talk about during this trip. "I'm really not. I had a happy childhood. I was never mad that you weren't around."

"I can only imagine the things your mom has said about me."

"She hasn't said anything bad," I said. "We never really talked about you until you called. She only said that you guys were very young and you got scared when she got pregnant and she was very sad that you left but she moved on."

"When you get older you will realize that not everything your mom tells you is true."

"I know that," I said. "I'm just saying I'm not mad."

We arrived at the lobby and my dad made small talk with the counter people while I stood idly behind him. He chatted cheerfully with the attendant, asked her about her day, and complimented her blouse.

That summer, several months after the trip to Mexico, my dad invited me to stay with him in Los Angeles for a few weeks. He wanted to pick me up and drive the ten hours to his place. Jessica and Aaron were going to fly down to stay with us as well. My dad told me about a red vintage Chevy Impala that he had purchased a few years ago. He said he wanted me to have it, that he would give it to me if I got my driver's license. I happily agreed, and he said he would register me in driving school in L.A. while I was staying with him.

He picked me up at our house, and we drove south, listening to a David Sedaris book on tape.

"Isn't this guy great? I just love that story about all those tics he has."

"Yeah, he's really funny. I have some tics, too, so it's very relatable."

"You don't have tics like David Sedaris. You don't count everything like he does. Or wash your hands repeatedly."

"Right, but I do other stuff. Hand-washing is a really common compulsion but really anything could be a tic."

"Do not become a hypochondriac, Chelsea. Did your mom put these ideas in your head?"

"No. I went to the doctor and he said I have mild Tourette's or OCD."

"Oh, please," he said, sounding disgusted.

We stopped overnight at a hotel somewhere in the Bay Area. The next day he gave me a list of things to accomplish while he was out doing errands that were never explained to me. My uncle Jett had told my mom that my dad had bought and then resold some kind of secret online business at the peak of the dot-com bubble and that it had earned him a million dollars. This explained his ability to travel and his apparent unemployment, but it didn't explain what we were doing in the Bay Area. But, like every other mystery he presented me with, I didn't ask.

My dad's list for me looked like this:

Talk to a stranger about your diet – 5 points
Do twelve pushups – 15 points
Read *Secrets of Professional Tournament Poker* by Jonathan Little for twenty minutes – 10 points
Spend $5.00 or more – 5 points
Eat a vegetable – 10 points
Ask a stranger a question – 10 points
Teach me how to do something – 10 points
Drink a glass of water – 5 points

The number of points each task was worth was equivalent to the dollar amount. I sensed that this was some kind of morality test to see if I would try to get as much money from him as possible, and felt sad and misunderstood.

When he came back, he asked me how the list was coming along and I told him about my accomplishments: I had eaten a carrot, I had spent five dollars on cashews and potato chips at the corner store, and I had consumed four glasses of water.

"How many points is that?" he said.

"Uh, thirty-five?" I said, pretending to do math in my head, having decided hours ago that thirty-five was a number of points that conveyed participation in his game but not so many points that it felt money-grubbing.

He tossed thirty-five one-dollar bills onto my bed. He was silent for the next couple of hours as he refolded the things in his suitcase and read the poker book. After a while he told me how disappointed he was that I hadn't worked harder on the list and hadn't completed more tasks.

"You didn't even offer to teach me anything," he said. "You could teach me anything. How you do your eye makeup, anything."

"Okay. Well, I don't normally just start telling people how to do things. It seems awkward. Why would you want to know how I did my eye makeup?" I said.

"I don't. Jesus. You need to meet me halfway here, Chelsea."

I tried to understand what the problem was. My dad wanted to change what I did and said, and also the way in which I did and said them, implying that possibly everything about me was, if not outright wrong, somehow off, in need of correction.

"Sorry," I said. "I don't know." I took a shower and went to bed, even though it was only 8:30 p.m. Then I lay awake trying to figure out where the problem had started. Was it because I didn't do everything on the list? Or was it because I balked at the idea of teaching him how I do my makeup? Maybe I needed to be more easygoing.

The next day we drove the rest of the way to Los Angeles. We hadn't talked much since the conversation about the list, and any conversation we attempted was strained and unsuccessful.

"Red Bull is made of bull semen," he said. "I don't care. I love it."

"Oh, weird. I used to drink a thing called Orbitz that had little balls floating in it."

"Um, okay."

At one point he exited the highway and pulled off onto the side of the road and we sat there in silence. I didn't know why we had stopped, or what was going to happen. I tried to appear relaxed and confident, open to stopping needlessly in the middle of a long drive without having to make a big deal about it, open to following his lead without understanding it or judging it.

I'm chill, I thought. *Stopping randomly on the highway and sitting here in silence is fine. This is actually a really chill spot.*

After about ten minutes, he pulled back onto the highway.

"Why didn't you ask me why I stopped?" he said half an hour later, irritation heavy in his voice.

"I don't know," I said, trying to sound chill. "I was fine with it."

"It's really starting to seem like you don't give a shit."

I began driving school on my second day in L.A. I enjoyed it, and I was very excited by the idea of having a car. I was always getting stranded in Clearlake, and if I wasn't stranded somewhere, I was stuck at home. With a car, I could do anything I wanted. Plus it was a beautiful car, big and solid and bright red. I took the written test and obtained a driver's permit and my dad let me drive the Impala around the block a couple of times. I was a little nervous and shaky, but I loved driving. I felt powerful and positive about the future.

Later, we went to the mall, where my dad shuttled me from store to store, picking out and purchasing preppy/sporty clothes for me that I knew I would never wear but which I allowed him to buy purely because of how surprised I was that someone would voluntarily spend so much money on me. He also bought me expensive makeup, and took me to get my hair done, deciding that I needed platinum-blonde highlights. It was all very impressive, though it was embarrassing to find out that I was so obviously in need of changing my appearance and style.

"I could tell the hairdresser thought I was some old creep, and that you were my girlfriend," he said.

"I don't think she thought that," I said.

"Are you kidding? That's definitely what she thought. She was looking at me weird the entire time."

"Okay," I said. "Well, maybe you could have said something like, *This is my daughter.*"

"You should just try to call me 'Dad' more frequently in public."

A few days later, my dad suggested that we go get colonics together. He promised that it would help with my acne, that it would release toxins that were trapped in my digestive system that were making it hard for my body to cleanse itself, that I would feel better immediately, and that my hair would be shinier. I felt hesitant. I told him I didn't want to do it. He said he knew of a good place, and gave me a binder full of laminated printouts of web pages about the importance of colon health and the positive impact of colon hydrotherapy.

"I'm sure it's cool, but I just don't feel ready to do that," I said. "Maybe next time?"

"Chelsea, you need to stop punishing me. Just look at the binder," he said. "But do not, under any circumstance, look at the last page of the binder." Then he left the house for several hours.

The printouts were incredibly boring and from clearly biased articles, and the whole "don't look at the final page" setup was extremely annoying, but I obediently skimmed through the colon hydrotherapy propaganda, avoiding the forbidden final page. Whatever eternal mysteries about my father or colonic health might have been solved had I looked at that page, I'll never know.

I looked at the photographs of fecal matter mixed with water and white orbs of plaque, resigning myself to the fact that this would play out like that dumb TV trope where someone says they are definitely not going to do something and then it cuts to them doing exactly what they said they were definitely not going to do.

The lady administering my colonic was Asian and spoke very little English. She gestured at the machine and asked me if I had any questions. I had learned from the binder that a colonic involves pumping water into one's colon and allowing it to mix with the remnants of your digestive tract, and then releasing that mixture out through the same tube and into some kind of shit machine. I told her I didn't have any questions, wanting to quickly get this over with. I was nervous and irritated, but she attempted to calm me by making unceasing eye contact with me as she slid the lubricated tube into my anus.

I could feel cool water entering my body, and I could feel it press against the inside of my stomach. At first I felt okay with it, and then I began feeling bloated, and then I felt sick, and then I felt very sweaty and nauseated and desperate for a toilet.

"Relack," the lady said. "Nothing come out yet. You need relack." I tried to relax. I tried to keep breathing, but I was too sweaty and nauseous and was becoming disoriented. The machine wasn't working. The water wasn't leaving my body the way it was supposed to. I was afraid I was going to pass out.

"Help," I said, squirming, trying to explain my situation. "I can't . . ."

She seemed mildly concerned and mildly pissed.

"Something is wrong," I said, aware that my line of vision was narrowing, somewhat sarcastically hoping to die.

"You need go, huh?" she said. I nodded. She pulled the tube out of my anus and I ran to the toilet on the other side of the room, watery poo dripping down my legs. I released into the toilet and started silently weeping while thinking *I don't understand, I don't understand* over and over, in reference to what felt like every single thing in the entire fucking universe.

"It's okay. I can do that," I said, still seated on the toilet as the woman wiped liquid poo off my legs. The woman continued to clean me anyway. I felt grateful that I didn't have to speak to communicate with her, that she could tell what I needed without my having to say it.

"Smell like ol' shit," she said accusingly.

My dad dropped me off at his house after the colonic and left to do another unexplained errand. Jessica and Aaron had been hanging out alone for most of the day and seemed bored. Aaron was blasting Ludacris from the giant living room stereo system with the bass turned all the way up. The sound penetrated the entire house. I was headachey, still nauseated, and emotionally exhausted, and I demanded, probably very impolitely, that Aaron turn the music down. We fought about it for several minutes before he pushed me out of the room and locked the door, preventing my access to the stereo. Shitty, stupid, bass-y music vibrated even louder through the entire house, and I felt myself becoming consumed by blind rage. I did what I still stubbornly believe was the best thing to do in my situation: I went to the bedroom the three of us were sharing and dragged Aaron's suitcase into the bathroom. I picked out each individual article of clothing, dropped it into the toilet, flushed, and threw it into the bathtub. It would have been equally effective to throw the clothes into the tub and turn the shower on, but I was committed to the toilet bowl process. Jessica watched me as I completed my task, then went and told Aaron what I had done. Aaron chased me around the house and then outside, eventually catching me between a car and a large prickly bush, punched me in the stomach, and pushed me backward into the bush. Capitalizing on the fact that I was stuck in the bush, he punched me a couple more times and then called me a "faggot," and went back into the house.

When my dad came home, he calmly listened to each of our stories and then asked me to wash the clothes I had stuffed into the toilet. I refused to do it, amazed at the suggestion that I do so. My dad said that he would really like it, and that it would really mean a lot to him, if I washed Aaron's clothes.

"There's no way I'm going to do that," I said after carefully considering the request. I was not going to apologize for my behavior. I didn't regret it. Maybe I was weird, or stupid, or irreparably frustrating to be around, or fundamentally unlovable. Maybe I would never overcome the obstacle of my own personality and for the rest of my life I would continue to slide helplessly into a pit of failure that was my own making. But I was not going to apologize for it.

"Okay, if you're sure," he said.

I confirmed that I was sure with no change in my voice or demeanor that might indicate to him that I had heard in his answer an implied disapproval of my personality. I wanted to suggest that I had an unlimited, insatiable capacity for disapproval, that there was no limit to the disapproval I could withstand. Then, for the first time in my life, I cried in front of my dad.

Later that evening I heard him apologize to Aaron on my behalf, and told him he would wash the clothes himself. Rozanna grunted and sighed unselfconsciously in the kitchen as she did the dishes. They were some of the most feminine noises I have ever heard. I wished I could be a woman like her, seemingly so unworried about how her presence affected anyone, calmly doing dishes in her own world. What does it feel like to be so self-assured? From the sleeping bag on the floor where I had been crying in for the last several hours, I fantasized about hugging her.

It sounds overly simplistic to say that I had a lot riding on the term *father*, that this was instrumental in my decision to talk to him, to continue being around him when I didn't have much to say, to cry pathetically when I didn't get preferential treatment from him over a child with less shared DNA. It was becoming clear that I was never going to have a *father* in the sense of the term as I understood it. There was no term for *adult who one meets as a teenager and clearly doesn't get along with but tries to, and ultimately fails, but keeps trying to form a bond with anyhow*, but apparently that was all I was going to get.

The next morning he told me he had reconsidered giving me the Impala.

"I don't think you're mature enough for a car," he said. "I'm going to sell it. I could get good money for that thing. You have no idea. It's a classic car."

"That's fine," I said, without looking at him.

I was disappointed, but I had been disappointed many times before, and I knew that disappointment was a feeling that not only fades but also makes future disappointments more bearable. Like many other things, disappointment gets easier with practice, and so, in that sense, this particular feeling of disappointment was ultimately worthwhile, an investment in my future of easier-to-handle-through-sheer-routine disappointments.

“I love you,” he said, seemingly out of nowhere.

“I love you, too,” I said, because I had never heard that expression from someone I didn’t love, and I didn’t know any other answer.

11

HOW TO BULLSHIT

Because only a very small part of me wanted to move away from my friends and family, I applied to just one very expensive art college, figuring I would most likely not be accepted, and, if I were, I would not be able to pay for it and therefore couldn't attend. Then it wouldn't be entirely my fault when I inevitably got pregnant my first year out of high school and lived in blissful, blameless poverty and squalor for the rest of my life.

College was not an obvious next step after high school in Clearlake. It seemed like a rare, special privilege meant only for the special and privileged. From each graduating class of about two hundred students at my high school, ten or twenty went to college directly after graduation. My family didn't encourage it much either. To us, it was something you might get around to after many years of work and raising children, and even then it was only night classes squeezed in after a full day's work.

So, out of caution, I remained ambivalent about my future. I was equally ready to leave town and go to college as I was to remain living at home and start my lifelong career at Safeway, where my aunt Helen could probably get me a job.

But I got accepted to the art school I applied to. And found a way to pay for it, sort of.

I got a small scholarship from my high school and a pretty good scholarship from the art school, and those, along with government loans each semester, would almost cover the cost of tuition. I took out a private student loan for $15,000 to cover the rest of tuition plus extra for rent, food, and art supplies. I knew that $15,000 wouldn't last four years, so I decided I would ride it out as long as possible, get part-time jobs to supplement that money, and figure out what to do when the money ran out.

I had never considered my family poor. In Clearlake, we had always occupied some middle ground between those who I now recognize were extremely poor, which was what I considered poor at the time, and those who were almost-not-poor, which was what I considered rich. In my mind, we were firmly middle class. This delusion was supported by the fact that we were able to rent a house with approximately enough bedrooms for everyone, that we ate dinner most nights, and that we were on welfare only when my mom was pregnant or nursing.

The first few months at art school dramatically changed my perception of where I fit in on the class scale. I was easily one of the poorest kids on campus. Of course there were other poors, like me. These were people taking on massive amounts of debt, who wouldn't allow themselves to purchase a cup of coffee, and who wore clothes their grandma had bought them before their freshman year of high school. The poors blended in pretty well, though. Art school is a great equalizer. Intentionally insane and disgusting attire was expected and encouraged, found objects counted as fine art, and eating cheap microwavable garbage was viewed as good time management. Plus, no one assumes you are poor when you're attending a college that costs $30,000 a year. No one is looking at you for clues of your poverty.

I watched and listened to my classmates carefully, waiting for them to drop clues of their wealth. A lot of them had been in art programs or art camps before attending college (things I hadn't had the luxury of even having heard of), and had flown around the country visiting schools to decide which program they most wanted to be in. A lot of them had parents who had encouraged their artistic interests by taking them to museums and buying them art supplies that were not available in Walmart. Some had parents who were artists themselves, who had fostered artistic thought in their children from a young age. Many of them didn't particularly want to be in art school, but had enough funds and pressure from their families to get a degree of some sort, and art school seemed like the easiest route for them to take.

I had so many questions about their wealth. Did they fly on private jets when they visited different campuses? Did they look at prices before ordering something from McDonald's? Was going to McDonald's something they even did? Did their families drink tap water or only sparkling bottled water? What was a trust fund? I didn't ask any of them, though, for fear of exposing my own undesirable economic status.

The initial awe and fascination with my privileged peers turned into anger and resentment halfway through my first semester, when I got my first job. I worked at a specialty tea café from 4 p.m. to midnight three nights a week. It was a cute café and I liked the job, but I became incredibly jealous of everyone who got to spend those twenty-four hours studying, visiting museums, working on art, and socializing. I already felt so behind artistically and academically, and now I had to work twice as hard to keep up.

I was spending the same amount of money on my education, but I wasn't really getting the same education. I couldn't spend every night in the studio, because I had to stand in front of a cash register and make bubble tea and pretend that these things filled me with such joy that I couldn't stop grinning and nodding supportively for my entire eight-hour shift. I couldn't read my assigned class materials thoroughly because I often had to do it after work the night before class. And if I realized halfway through a project that there was a more interesting way to do something, or I had a better idea, I couldn't afford to start the project over.

I knew these were rich-people problems. Only rich people could afford to complain about the lack of time they had to create still lifes of indoor flora and to read about Dadaists. Complaining about my rich-people problems made me feel whiny and spoiled and further separated me from my impoverished roots. I felt as hypocritical as the Dadaists themselves, who critiqued the materialistic bourgeoisie while making art that, like most art, only rich people had the resources to consume.

On the other hand, my problems weren't exactly rich-people problems. Sure, rich people might complain about a lack of time to finish Dada homework, but not because they were busy working a minimum-wage job. Rich people might use their extra time to attend the new show at MoMA, or to network with Sophie, whose mother ran an arts residency and was looking for applicants from our graduating class, but I was trying to earn money to buy enough frozen single-serving lasagnas from Safeway to get myself through the week. In this way, I also felt alienated from my new peers, unable to be as smart or productive or connected as they were because I had to attend to my basic needs.

I was in an economic no-man's-land, rich in education and opportunity, poor in money and time, with no one to complain to.

I took financial shortcuts wherever I could find them, stealing small portions of tea from my job after every shift, "dining out" at gallery openings every week, basing project ideas off of supplies I already had or could be stolen from the textiles department, and living in a bedroom the size of a medium-size closet. Then, inevitably, I'd have a weak moment, blow forty-five dollars at a fabric store, and make a mental note to beat myself up over it every time I made a student loan payment for the rest of my life.

I began to question my reasons for being in art school. Was I actually an artist? Was it worth the amount of money I was spending to figure it out? Did I need to be here even if I were an artist? And, if I wasn't an artist, what exactly was I doing? These are common questions for art students, rich or poor. It isn't easy to come to terms with the fact that artistically expressing intangibles is what you want to do with your life. It's amazing to me that teenagers are encouraged to make these kinds of long-lasting decisions about their futures, are given what seems at the time like play money to follow their whims, are manipulated into betting future income on what they feel like doing when they're seventeen or eighteen, ages deemed *years too young* to be responsible enough to handle alcohol.

I remained in art school because, as difficult and expensive as these questions were, I had no other ideas for my life. Obtaining an art degree was a vague, nearly meaningless goal, but it was the only one I had. I'd already invested so much just by enrolling that I was determined to find some value. Maybe the next class I took would be the one to change my life. Maybe when I graduated I would be offered a glamorous art job. Maybe I needed to trust whatever misguided impulse had brought me to art school and saddled me with an unfathomable amount of debt in the first year alone, to see this thing through until I was absolutely bankrupt.

I couldn't help but see each class I took as a dollar amount. I watched money borrowed from some hypothetical future self spill away as I tried to understand my poorly planned and ill-conceived academic and creative pursuits.

I took a $3,000 required drawing class and gained confidence drawing plants in charcoal.

I took a $3,000 Intro to 2-D Materials class that was mandatory for all students, and was required to do things like cut up pieces of paper and staple them to a tree and was reprimanded by my professor for not taking it seriously.

I took a $3,000 oil painting class and realized halfway through that I hated oil painting.

I took a $3,000 illustration class and a $3,000 intermediate illustration class and realized that maybe I didn't really like acrylic or watercolor painting that much either.

I enrolled in a $3,000 textiles class because two of my friends were taking it. I liked weaving, so the next semester I took a $3,000 weaving class and a $3,000 advanced weaving class and after those I took a $3,000 jacquard weaving class and realized that I couldn't imagine weaving for the rest of my life, that it seemed more like a relaxing hobby that I could do one day when I was rich enough to buy a loom and have studio space big enough to house it than an art form I was seriously interested in pursuing.

I took a $3,000 general writing class and loved it, so I took a $3,000 fiction writing class and a $3,000 literature class and a $3,000 creative nonfiction class, and was then told that I had taken classes in too many disciplines outside my declared major, painting, and would never graduate on time.

I was advised to finish my studies in painting, as I had almost enough painting and drawing credits to satisfy those graduation requirements. The writing and literature courses could be used to fulfill my humanities requirements. Or I could apply to be an interdisciplinary major, which would require me to convince a jury that my art practice was so nuanced and complicated that I needed the support of multiple departments. Unable to envision myself finishing school in the painting department, I chose the latter, even though I did not know how to present my work as interdisciplinary. Also, come to think of it: What work? The weavings I had abandoned the year before? The short stories I was just beginning to write? The paintings that I stopped making after my first year?

I was embarrassed that I had spent three years and more money than I could even conceptually fathom to figure out I didn't like painting, that I kind of liked weaving, and that I was interested in writing. My mistakes were adding up.

I had spent more money on my education than anyone in my family or town had ever led me to believe I should spend on anything. I didn't have the luxury of having a parent or society to blame for pressuring me to go to a fancy college. I had done this all on my own. I was to blame. I thought I could be an artist, but clearly I could not. Art was for rich people, people who could afford to take the time out of their lives to learn a craft, and I was financially ruining myself to learn this.

I felt guilty and stupid for attending such an expensive school when many of my high school friends were in community college waiting to transfer, or had already given up on the idea of college altogether and were still living with their parents, working at Walmart or the gas station or something. I was extremely lucky. I had so much privilege. Complaining even a little bit would be unappreciative and ignorant, I reminded myself. Over and over, I reminded myself how lucky I was.

I tried to stay confident and optimistic. Maybe I would have more to write and make art about than I would if money and experiences had been handed to me. Maybe there was some psychological benefit to working hard. Maybe my massive debt would be the fuel I needed to become a success. Maybe there were advantages to being poor. Maybe I was like the guy named Loser the *Freakonomics* guys wrote about, who was so burdened by his name that it became a motivating factor for making a good life for himself, surpassing his brother Winner in all standard measures of success. Maybe that was who I was—setting myself up to drown in debt so that I would have to become strong and have no choice but to succeed.

•

At the beginning of my last semester, I found out that my government loans had not been issued in the amount I expected, so I was $3,200 short on tuition. I was still working at the tea café and had also taken a nice-paying work-study job in the administration office, but my private loan money was gone, no one was helping me pay my bills, and there was no way I could afford a $3,200 payment on top of rent and bills and all the other grown-up things I was now responsible for.

"Is there some kind of extra loan I could get?" I asked my financial adviser. There seemed to be no limit to the amount of money I would steal from my future self. If my future self became financially successful, I figured, $3,200 would be nothing to her. And if she were unsuccessful and continued to be poor, the exact amount of her debt would be irrelevant, as it was already so high that she would only ever be able to make minimum payments, if that, for the rest of her life.

"You've taken out all the loans you qualify for," my adviser told me.

"Maybe I have to drop out," I said. I felt relieved at the thought, and also slightly badass, as if dropping out might add depth or authenticity to my personality, or harden me.

Yeah, that's me, I dropped out of art school, I would say defiantly to my friends at the homeless shelter, my voice somehow deep and dry from the existential heaviness of not obtaining an art degree. *Who's askin'?*

"You want to get your degree," my adviser said firmly. "You've already invested so much time and money, and you just have one semester left."

"What can I do?" I said.

"Is there anyone in your family you can borrow money from?" she said.

I imagined my seven-year-old sister holding a weekend bake sale or lemonade stand, and then imagined myself manipulating her into giving me the jar of quarters she earned. *You know I'm good for it,* I would say, my imaginary self in this scenario imagining an even less likely version of myself who was about to become rich from the sale of a piece of imaginary art, art that no imaginary version of myself could picture but that I knew must exist somewhere deep within me. I imagined bringing my sister's jar of quarters into my financial adviser's office and emptying it onto the desk. *Plenty more where that came from*, I would say, unsure why I was using a threatening tone of voice.

"No," I said. "Nobody has any money."

"Okay." She sighed. "Think about it over the weekend and come back in on Monday."

I avoided my financial adviser's office and any phone call from an unknown number after that, hoping my tuition shortage would be forgotten.

I pulled together my interdisciplinary presentation. My weavings were actually illustrations, I explained to the jury, because I used the color and composition methods that I learned in my studies in painting and applied those concepts to the weavings. Illustration is imagery shown alongside or instead of text, and it just so happened that my weavings, when paired with their descriptions, sort of formed a satirical narrative about societal pressures. I printed books that reproduced my art next to short essays I wrote about their meaning, in case the connection to writing wasn't clear.

"You're so irreverent," one of the jurors said, smiling.

It turns out being an art student while struggling to pay my bills taught me a very important life lesson after all: how to bullshit.

I spent my last semester finishing my requirements and taking writing classes. For my senior show, I recited a long poem I had written called "McDonald's Is Impossible," which I had memorized. I served McDonald's French fries and hamburgers, which I had cut up into hors d'oeuvre–size quarters and placed elegantly on platters.

After graduation, instead of receiving a diploma, I received a bill from the school in the amount I owed. I didn't pay it, reasoning that I would try to cough up the money if it turned out I needed a piece of paper proving I had a BFA.

I have never had a reason to see proof of my academic achievement.

12

MAN-HATER

Mornings before I went to work, if I had time, I would stop at James's house and cuddle with him in his bed for half an hour. I cherished this time with him. I loved his soft, nearly motionless kisses and I loved being held by his warm sleepy body. Usually I couldn't fall asleep, so I would lie there and stare at him, maybe try to move a chunk of his dark hair away from his face without waking him up. I also loved the fact that in the early morning, when he was hours away from being fully conscious, I was free of the responsibility of talking to him.

I had broken up with James months earlier over the phone, when I was living two hours away in Oakland during my first year of art school and he was in Clearlake and still a senior in high school. We had started dating right before the school year ended and had a happy, fun summer together, but once I left for college, the relationship became a chore. I would have liked to see James every day, but since that was impossible, it seemed easier and less frustrating just to give up on our relationship altogether and reallocate the hours I spent on the phone with him each night doing other things—making friends, pursuing other romances, and honing my artistic skills.

But this isn't what I said to James when I broke up with him. I told him it was his personality that drove me away.

"You're becoming too needy," I said, trying to speak into the phone loudly enough so that he would hear me over his own crying, but not so loud that I would be heard through the walls of my dorm room. "You call me too much."

I continued talking to him on the phone every night for weeks after our breakup, implying that I was trying to tend to his feelings of broken-heartedness but mostly trying to lessen the emotional repercussions the breakup was causing me: guilt, loneliness, and the nagging thought that I would never find anyone else willing to tolerate my personality as eagerly as he did. I had the feeling that the world was suddenly expanding at an emotionally overwhelming rate, making me feel tiny and insignificant and seeming to call into question my purpose, especially late at night while I did things like glue dried leaves onto an incredibly shitty "natural materials" 3-D Design project that was due the next morning. Talking to James made me feel grounded, and even if our conversations were awful and confusing and emotionally draining, it seemed right to be going through this together.

"It is so much easier to be the person broken up with," I told him, using a tone of condescending maturity that I found annoying even while I was using it. "Someday you'll understand what I'm going through and you'll feel bad that you gave me such a hard time."

When I finally started feeling good about being single and didn't need his emotional support anymore, I demanded he stop calling me. I had other shit going on, I explained. I could not be expected to prioritize the needs of my long-distance ex-boyfriend indefinitely. I had art openings and parties to attend, projects to work on. Just taking the time to explain this to him was eating into my college experience.

"I am literally passing up opportunities to hang out with people so that you can have the privilege of listening to the same annoyed, half-hearted explanation of this situation for the fifty-fourth time," I said.

But once my first year was over and I was back in Clearlake for the summer, James and I fell quickly into old habits. We hung out constantly, made out in front of our friends, took turns drawing each other's portraits, talked about music and art and the future, and gave each other back massages. I clumsily avoided conversations about our relationship, and when he backed me into a corner about it, we fought.

"We do everything we did when we were together. And you tell me you still love me. So why can't I be your boyfriend?" he would say.

"You're making me regret coming over," I would say, arms folded, staring into his watery eyes until he submitted to my will and looked away.

I knew I was behaving poorly, but I had already decided to forgive myself. I was being selfish and shitty and irresponsible with the feelings of someone I claimed to care about, but I was a teenager. I was allowed to make mistakes. Wasn't that the whole point of being a teenager? Surely, as a teenager, I was entitled to choose when to ignore and when to capitalize on my ex-boyfriend's feelings, based exclusively on what would be most beneficial to my own needs while preserving the image of myself as a sensitive human being. Surely I was allowed to bend the shape of reality in my own mind to make it something I could comfortably live within.

Surely, I thought, no one would begrudge a teenager the right to make a few mistakes.

The trap of Clearlake is financial as much as it is geographical as much as it is psychological. Being born there all but guarantees a life of poverty. Getting finances together to move out of town is a huge obstacle. Mountains surround Lake County, where Clearlake is nestled, and on the other side are places like Napa and St. Helena, towns that cater to the very rich and offer few incentives for poor people to visit or move into. Beyond those towns are modest cities like Santa Rosa, which you might, if you were a very privileged Clearlake resident, visit a few times a year when you wanted to go to the mall. But many people don't leave town very often, and this creates a fear of the outside world that only becomes more pronounced as time goes on.

Some people try to leave. They go to college, or move in with a relative in some nearby city, or pack up everything and just go. My mom and Seth and I had done this when I was seven; we'd packed up a U-Haul and moved to Washington state to start over. We enjoyed some adverse weather, discovered Starbucks, and started obsessively collecting and trading stickers with our new friends. (Okay, that was probably just me.) But Clearlake beckoned, so we drove our U-Haul back before I turned eight. It was a sad, fucked-up little town with absolutely no opportunity, but it was ours. These were our dirt roads. These were the crackheads we had known our whole lives.

It was funny how beautiful Clearlake now appeared to me after a year of being away at college. It was as if I had never really looked at it before. Maybe it was that I had spent the year in a large, dirty city and was grateful to be away from the frenzy and constant light. Maybe it was that I had just spent the year making art and wondering why I was making art and being asked to defend my artistic choices in front of people who seemed to have a much better idea of why they were making art than I did, and it was just such a relief to be around simple, artless people who didn't want to hear about that stuff and only wanted to get drunk with me.

Or maybe I was beginning to feel Clearlake's pull, the one that no one can seem to escape, the persistent voice that told me life was better here, that maturity was being able to see the majestic rolling hills without being bothered by the smoky, rotting trailers that peppered them. That maybe this was the only place in the world where I could stand out as special. That maybe I belonged here.

•

"Do you still love me?" James said as I detached myself from him and his bed, checking myself in the mirror to make sure my uniform wasn't too wrinkled.

Of course I knew what James meant when he asked me if I loved him, and I knew what it meant that he even felt he needed to ask. It meant that I was successfully manipulating him. It meant that I was maintaining his love and attention while avoiding any of the responsibility that I felt when we were in a legitimate relationship.

But I pretended to believe he meant *Do you love me?* in the broader sense of love that included the love I had for my brother, for example, or my cat, or sesame seed bagels with extra cream cheese, which I did love, without a doubt. I loved him very much in that sense of the word, and told him so in that quick, irritated way that implied that any further questioning on the matter would lead to a fight.

On days I didn't have to work, James and I would go to parties, or have friends over to James's house. Otherwise he would come over and hang out with my family at my uncle Jett's house.

I had met Uncle Jett the previous year, at the same time I'd met my dad, his brother. My mom had recently separated from her husband, Seth, and Jett had recently divorced his wife. It was a match made in incest-joke heaven, and by the time I left for college, my mom was breaking the lease at our house and she and my siblings were moving into the house Jett's wife and kids had just moved out of.

My friends were careful to avoid asking me too much about this situation, probably for fear of making me feel like a hillbilly, so I had to come up with most of my own incest jokes: "My uncledad and auntmom are picking my siblingcousins up from school"; "I am my own favorite cousin."

Jett was argumentative, and cunning in that way where you felt as if you were about to be tricked into saying something that would prove his point. I liked these traits at first. It was fun to argue with someone who was so good at it. But it got old quickly. He wanted to argue about everything, and was stubborn and defensive when you didn't back down. He talked this way with my brother and sister, who were nine and six, and it bothered me.

"Yes," he would say to them, "you guys can go play on the trampoline, absolutely. But you have to sweep off the deck first. Why? Because you two played on the deck yesterday and leaves have blown onto it since then and you have to help take care of the things you use."

It was difficult to argue with that. The fact that sweeping the deck hadn't been mentioned before the minute they wanted to do something else was annoying, but it was his house, they were just kids, and it had a certain kind of logic.

But this deal-making was constant. Oh, they wanted to play video games in the living room? They had to give two reasons Jett should have to listen to video game noises on his day off.

"Mom said we could," River tried.

"That doesn't address my issue with the noise."

"They can play with the sound off," I offered.

"That's not the point," Jett said.

Well, what the fuck is the point, I thought, but I let it go.

I was trying to like Jett. I had hated Seth for so long, had begged my mom to leave him for years. And Seth had left us several times over the years, to stay with his mom or uncle for a few blissful weeks, but it never stuck. He always came back. I wanted so badly for my mom's relationship with Jett to work so that Seth would never, ever come back. Plus, I didn't want to be the kind of person who hated everyone my mom dated.

But even when Jett was doing something nice, there was an aggressiveness to his approach.

"I'm going to give you some money when you go back to school," Jett said to me one day, out of nowhere.

"Oh, that's okay," I said. "I'll be fine."

"If I don't, then your mom will have to, since I'm guessing you aren't planning on working during the school year, and you'll probably need books and supplies, and your mom and I are sharing money anyway, so it's all the same to me."

"I'm saving money. And actually I am planning on working during the school year. I worked last semester."

"You don't have to argue with me. I'm trying to be nice. I'm doing you a favor. Not everything has to be a debate."

"Okay," I said. "Well, thank you. That is nice."

Jett often called me a "man-hater," and though I saw through it as an offensive tactic to get me to act more amiably towards him, it was a tactic that sort of worked. Being called a man-hater filled me with a frustration that I did not dare express, for fear that the expression of my rage would be turned back towards me and repackaged as more man-hating.

It was true that I hated Seth, and, yes, I was beginning to hate Jett and my dad. But this was such an unfair sample pool! Was I really expected to like everybody my mom had ever been attracted to? Didn't other men count?

I liked my grandpa. I liked my high school ceramics teacher. I liked James. With them I didn't feel any of the anxiety or resentment I felt towards Jett or Seth or my dad. But Jett's words still nagged me. Did I *really* care about these men I claimed to care about? What had I ever done to indicate that I really cared? Did I ever call my grandpa on the phone, or try to talk to him when we visited, or did I mostly just talk to my grandma and aunts? Had I kept in touch with my high school ceramics teacher who I claimed to be so attached to? Had I bothered to send the thank-you card I wrote for him before graduation, explaining how important he was to me and how much he helped me in my decision to go to college? Or had I forgotten, found the card months later in a stack of old school paper, and never tried to contact him again?

Did I really give a shit about James? Did I? Was I treating him like he was a person I cared about? Or was using him to quell my feelings of inadequacy and loneliness more important to me than being clear about where our relationship stood so that he could decide to move on?

Jett and my mom fought passionately and regularly. It reminded me of my mom's fights with Seth. There was the same throwing of heavy sentimental objects, the same pushing and slapping of each other. Doors slamming and then doors opening for the sake of dramatic re-slamming. Yelling. But Jett was a lot sharper than Seth had ever been. He berated my mom with crazy nonsense framed as logic that was purposefully designed to misdirect, provoke, and confuse her.

"No, you started the argument," he would say. "You were yelling at me from the bedroom before I had said anything about the money you owe me. I remember very clearly because I couldn't hear what you were saying because I was warming up pizza in that piece-of-shit microwave you brought over, and I couldn't leave it alone to come talk to you because River was in the kitchen and he eats any scrap of food left unattended for more than two minutes. It's disrespectful and you know it. My son never ate like that."

Another big difference between these fights and her fights with Seth was Jett's excessive drinking and my mom's moderate (but very new, and therefore somewhat unpredictable) drinking.

One night, my mom either fell or was pushed down a flight of stairs. She and Jett had both been drinking. Scared, not really knowing what to do, I shuffled my mom and my siblings into my mom's car and drove us around the mostly empty back roads that I usually took when I drove to James's house, waiting until my mom sobered up or we thought of somewhere we could go.

"Just go to Nana and Papa's," my mom yelled from the backseat.

"I can't. I have work in the morning," I said. "I don't have my uniform."

When the gas light came on, I decided we would go back to Jett's house to grab my mom's purse and my work uniform, and then drive the forty-five minutes to Nana's house. Before we could make it back, though, we were pulled over by a cop who had been looking for us. Jett had called 911, claiming he had been given a black eye. My mom was taken to jail on domestic abuse charges while I was left in her car with my brother and sister. I was never asked, for the record, if I had a driver's license. (I didn't.)

I drove us straight to our nana and papa's house without picking up my uniform or my mom's purse, hoping that we could make it without stopping for gas, for which I had no money. I called in sick the next day, unable to work without my uniform and unable to get my uniform from Jett's house without having to face Jett.

"I cannot believe your mom is dating that fucking asshole," James said when I called him.

"Fucking marry me," I said.

"What?" he said.

I could see that I was becoming a little overconfident about my ability to manipulate James and was losing my touch for subtlety. That, or he was no longer desperately looking for proof that I loved him.

"I just mean that you're right. It seems like nobody else gets it. I appreciate you."

"Don't say things like that."

"Okay, I won't. I won't say anything at all. I'll just sit here quietly and behave myself."

"Come on, Chelsea."

"No, it's fine. I have better things to do than give you compliments all day."

I got an email from my dad saying that if I wanted him to give me money for school I should ask him directly instead of contriving a situation where Jett would have to give me money if my dad didn't, and that I should be more sensitive about my dad's relationship with his brother, which, he explained, had historically been tenuous but was now in an even more fragile state, given Jett's relationship with my mom and my living with them for the summer, which made him feel insecure, not that he didn't fully support them as a couple, because he did, and I should too.

"Forget it," I wrote back. "I don't need money from anyone. I didn't even ask Jett for money. It was his idea and I said no but he kept insisting and I didn't want to be rude."

"Why did you tell your dad you didn't need money?" Jett asked me. "Why should I pay for your books if your dad is offering to pay for them?"

"I don't know. You really shouldn't. I don't want you to. I'm not asking anybody to pay for school. I don't understand you people."

"We're all just trying to help you. You can at least be gracious."

James and I convinced his family to let me stay with them for a week. We told them I wasn't getting along with my family; we possibly even lied and said that Jett had kicked me out. James's parents didn't particularly like the idea of us having sleepovers, but because James had two twin beds in his room, they were able to suspend their disbelief in regard to the power of teenage hormones.

Being with James all the time felt good. Time seemed infinite, so there was very little pressure to resolve any of our issues.

James didn't ask me if I loved him, but I told him I did anyway. I wanted him to know that I cared about him, that he was more than an appendage to me, that I wasn't a man-hater, that I respected him, that I was tired of being destructive.

James's friend Cameron began messaging me on Myspace. He said that he had heard about me from James and had seen me around high school the year before and thought we should be friends. I remembered seeing him around school too. He was scruffy and quiet and seemed to be interested only in hanging out with his girlfriend. His Myspace headline was Gimme Minnie, which I thought was clever and adorable. Minnie, I knew, was his longtime girlfriend.

Cameron was an unusually forward friend, suggesting we exchange numbers and "hang out sometime" within the first hour of our communication. He started picking me up after work and taking me to Minnie's parents' house, where both he and Minnie were living. We would watch movies, eat macaroni and cheese prepared by Minnie's mom, and sleep in sleeping bags on the floor. Kraft macaroni and cheese was Cameron's idea of health food. He ate almost nothing but fast food, primarily from Taco Bell, and it was rumored that he defecated only once per week. This rumor, which was at some point confirmed by Cameron, somehow factored in positively to the crush I was developing on him.

"You need to cut your mom and Jett some slack," my dad wrote in an email. "I know you think it's weird that your mom is dating your uncle but it's actually pretty funny if you think about it. He's your 'uncledad.' Haha. Have a sense of humor, Chelsea."

I had never made any indication that I had a problem with my mom dating my uncle on the basis that he was my uncle, and I already found both the term and concept *uncledad* pretty funny. I had made and laughed at that joke months ago—so many times, in fact, that it wasn't funny anymore.

His implication that I had some kind of superficial, hillbilly-phobic problem with my mom dating my uncle was unfair. The fact that Jett was my uncle didn't preclude my having an unfavorable opinion about him as a person. Jett was a dick, a bully, occasionally violent, definitely vindictive, stubborn, arrogant, drank too much, and was as full of shit as my dad was. I had no reason to like Jett.

I didn't answer the email.

The next day I got another email from my dad. "Are you mad at me? You're going to have a hard life if you get mad at people this easily. Write back if you care."

"I'm not mad," I wrote.

I was beyond mad. I was sick of these grown adult men projecting their problems and insecurities onto me. I was sick of being expected to believe that these strange, fucked-up people were members of my family and therefore deserved my respect, when they had disregarded my existence for my entire childhood. I was sick of being bullied into believing that if I didn't automatically love and admire every man that was presented to me, that meant that I hated all men.

I wasn't a man-hater. I was an asshole-hater. I was a shithead-hater. I hated people for who they were. I was a person-hater. This was equal opportunity. It wasn't my fault that many of the shitheads currently in my life were men. That was not my problem.

Cameron and Minnie broke up. I can't remember the details, but I don't think it had anything to do with me. After their breakup, Cameron and I started hanging out more. We would make out, drive around in his car, try to think of things to talk about, eat Taco Bell, and, ultimately, one night in the Taco Bell parking lot with a taco twelve-pack and a Nachos Supreme, we discussed whether or not we should have sex.

"You're going to have to talk to James," I said in my infinite wisdom.

"What do you mean?" Cameron said.

"I can't do it if he's not okay with it. He'll hate both of us forever."

"I don't know if it's a good idea to tell him," he said, probably simultaneously weighing the pros and cons of continuing to engage with my faulty sense of logic.

"He's going to find out anyway," I said, fully believing my own phony, manipulative reasoning. "Things will turn out much better if you're straightforward with him from the outset."

Cameron told me he would call James the next day.

James called me after Cameron talked to him, wanting to know what exactly was going on, whether I did or did not love him, saying something about betrayal. I yelled at him for being mad at Cameron, for not dealing with his feelings in a mature and rational way, and for telling Cameron he didn't want him to sleep with me, as I deduced had happened. I was shopping for fabric in Walmart as I quiet-yelled at James on the phone, told him that he was embarrassing me, and that, as an artist, I needed to be able to shop for art supplies without having to counsel my jealous ex-boyfriend.

"You said you loved me," he said. "You wouldn't do this if that were true."

"Both can be true," I said firmly.

I called Cameron and told him that it didn't matter what James had said, that I wanted to sleep with him anyway.

We went to Cameron's mom's trailer, where she made us fried bologna and cheese sandwiches, and then Cameron and I attempted to have sex in a smaller trailer outside of her regular trailer. Cameron was slim, so I was surprised by how much loose skin he had on his stomach and legs. I thought of all the Taco Bell we had eaten together in the last few weeks, how the fat cells from those meals were accumulating in the skin that was now touching my skin, and all the poop he probably currently had gathered in his body.

I was repulsed, not just by his body, but by myself for thinking that having sex with this strange, unhealthy person that I was only marginally interested in was somehow worth the pain it might cause another person. A person I liked. A person who had always been really great to me. Maybe the only person I had talked to all summer who hadn't tried to manipulate me or make me feel bad, even though he was the only person who had good reason to.

Cameron and I struggled to guide his penis into my vagina for a little while before I gave up, saying, "I'm bored." After a little while, I asked him to drive me home.

•

"I'm coming to Clearlake," my dad wrote in an email.

The thought of him visiting worried me. But still, despite myself, I thought there was a chance it might go well. That he would finally realize how special and worthy of his attention I was. I wanted to be told that he regretted not being around to watch me grow up. That I deserved to have had a dad and that he was sorry for not giving that to me. That he would give anything to have spent just one day with me as a child. I wanted to hear him say that things were hard between us now because we were both so bull-headed and self-protective and because so much time had passed, but that things would get better, that we would learn to love each other, that we would someday feel like real family.

"Your mom is threatening to throw my coins in the river," the email went on, "and Jett seems to be backing her up, so expect me in 24–48 hours to pick them up. You can forget about me helping you with school money if your mom destroys those coins."

Then the email quoted a lengthy email exchange between him and Jett about speakers and storage spaces and how pathetic it was that Jett still lived in Clearlake and how selfish it was for my dad to have lived in France at some point, none of which seemed to involve me in any way. I wasn't sure why it had been quoted to me.

"What coins?" I asked my mom.

"Oh, Jesus Christ," she said. "Did your dad call you?"

"He emailed."

"Jett showed me some coins that your dad gave him for safekeeping a long time ago, and I joked and said I was going to throw them in the lake and Jett got mad at me and now I guess he talked to your dad about it."

But my dad never came to Clearlake, and the coin issue remained unresolved. Over time the issue turned into verbal artillery used by each party at his own convenience, rarely face-to-face or even directly referred to, but rather alluded to in conversations and one-liners so far from the original point that it was as if language had adapted to accommodate the complex and loaded implications of the words *coins* and *river* and *France* for the explicit benefit of allowing each party to verbally attack the other without having to actually bring up the issue directly.

After a week, I called James. I told him that it was important to me that he wasn't mad at me, and for him to know that I knew I had fucked up. That I wouldn't be able to live with myself if I had ruined our friendship. That I had never cared about someone as much as I cared about him, but that I also cared about myself and needed time to figure out what I wanted. I hadn't apologized, but at some point I stopped talking, waiting to be forgiven.

"I have something to say too," James said.

"Okay."

"I hung out with Marcy a few times. We hooked up."

Marcy was once my best friend in high school, but it was a troubled friendship and we drifted apart as it became exceedingly clear that she was happiest when I felt rejected.

I felt my body flush with a level of humiliation previously unknown to me. Suddenly I had lost the one thing that I thought was unconditionally mine.

"You're disgusting," I said calmly. "You're fucking so disgusting that I think I might get off the phone right now so I can go vomit."

"Shut up. That's not fair."

"I'm never touching you again. Also, you should really get tested."

I didn't have any reason to believe Marcy had a disease, but I thought it was the meanest thing I could say, and I wanted to cover up the pain I was feeling. I was upset, but it wasn't James's fault. I had made this mess for myself, with selfishness and hypocrisy and manipulation and carelessness. I had been using James to create drama that I could control to shield myself from the pain caused by the drama other people were creating and controlling around me, and it wasn't working anymore.

We both cried helplessly into the phone, knowing that this was the end of whatever we had been doing.

I cried all night, called in sick to work the next morning, and was fired for it the day after. My behavior was unprofessional and irresponsible, I was told. I was simply not cut out to bag groceries full-time in a small town I on-again, off-again resented.

I counted down the days until my return to art school, longing for the simple pleasure of spending all night on an art project I would immediately throw away after the class critique.

I realized the point of being assigned to glue leaves to paper. No one could create anything interesting with such materials with a one-day turnaround, and therefore we had all been assigned to present literal garbage, pretending that it was emotionally driven or artistically significant. We had to stand in front of our peers and talk about our garbage, get our teacher on board with the meaning of our garbage, hear ourselves say out loud that it was caused by some burning creative force inside of us. The garbage of our lives.

The point was to internalize the garbage. Even when we threw it out immediately after class, it was there in the backs of our minds, in our body of work, reminding us of the shit that we were capable of. We had to accept what we had done, find something useful in it, and move on.

13

TRASHY COMING-OF-AGE STORY

During my second year in college, my mom broke up with Jett, and she and my siblings moved out of his house and into a mansion. It was cheaper than renting a regular house, my mom said, but the catch was that the owner of the mansion sometimes lived there, too, so there were parts of the mansion that would be off-limits to my family.

"Are you sure it's safe to live with a stranger?" I said. "It's probably worth it to just rent a regular house that you can have to yourselves."

"It's fine. He said he's hardly ever going to be there."

The other catch, which was actually more of a perk, was that the mansion was filled with stuff. The owner had just purchased the house, and the previous owner seemed to have not taken any of her belongings with her when she left. There was a living room with couches and tables and plants, and a movie room with theater curtains and a movie projector. There was a pool table in the den. The drawers and cupboards were filled with expensive trinkets and old jewelry and dishes and batteries. The various workrooms stored outdated printers and fax machines and sewing machines and craft and hobby supplies of all kinds. The garage had bikes and fishing gear and tool chests and garden equipment and pool toys.

It was like walking through an estate sale where everything is suddenly yours.

"I'll be taking these," I said to my mom, putting a bunch of sewing supplies into my backpack.

"Sure," she said. "I doubt the new owner even knows what's here."

I had never been much of a thief. My cousin and I stole some hair clips from Walmart when I was ten and, feeling guilty, immediately told my mom what we had done. "Be careful," was all she'd said. The next year, I regularly stole giant Mr. Goodbar and Symphony bars from the grocery store near my elementary school, shoving them into the lining of my corduroy jacket. After that I lost interest in stealing. It didn't seem worth the risk and I didn't like candy that much.

But being in my mom's rental mansion was like being in Aladdin's Cave of Wonders. The endless bounty of random objects technically belonged to the mansion's owner, but there was too much stuff to keep track of, and none of it was being used. Plus, the owner was, as he'd promised, never around, and it didn't feel like stealing if I was taking things from a house my mom lived in.

Whenever I visited, I stole a few little things. A couple skeins of yarn. A basket. Cleaning supplies. Some silverware. A road bike. A digital sewing and embroidery machine. A serger. Some kind of land-surveying equipment that I didn't understand but that looked valuable and sellable.

And a can of air duster.

At parties I had done whippets, from small cans of nitrous oxide, and thought the duster would feel the same, but the duster was more intense and the effect seemed to last slightly longer. I inhaled deeply, and—briefly, beautifully—lost all my connections to the world. I could see and hear and control my body, but nothing meant anything to me. I didn't hold any associations. It ended a few seconds after it began, and I would feel completely normal again. I could read, or cook, or do any number of normal activities. But what I did most often was hit the can again, and again, and again. I loved how the blankness felt. I loved being free, completely free, of my anxieties, for even a few seconds.

I knew very quickly that the can of duster was a problem. As much as I loved the feeling it gave me, I was also terrified by how great it felt, how easy it was, how accessible.

"The feeling you're getting is the feeling of losing hundreds of brain cells simultaneously," friends told me. And, "You're going to become brain-dead."

The can of duster lasted forever. I was afraid it would never run out, but I couldn't bear to throw it away. I took it to Oakland and encouraged my friends to try it, wanting to share it but also wanting for it to be consumed more quickly and be out of my life. I started hiding it from myself, and making rules about when and how I could use it: only if someone else also wanted to use it, and even then only ten times in a row at the most. But I found it difficult to follow these rules, and often I would come home drunk and take a few hits by myself, my drunkenness adding nothing to the experience except a lack of self-control.

On one of the many weekends I found myself in Clearlake, my friend Brandon picked me up at my mom's rental mansion and drove us around aimlessly in his little car. Brandon was one of the few friends from high school I still kept in touch with. Though we rarely talked, and saw each other even less, he felt kindred to me, and each time I saw him it was as if no time had passed.

There were two kinds of people who grew up in our town: people who never considered ever leaving Clearlake, and people who left as quickly as possible and spent the rest of their lives trying to distance themselves from it. Brandon and I were both the second type. Brandon had moved to San Diego after high school but moved back after a year, and was making plans to leave again. I didn't ask him much about it, not wanting to embarrass him. I was in Oakland but coming back to visit at every opportunity, never knowing why I was still most comfortable hanging out in a town I had so eagerly escaped.

We stopped on the side of the road where there was a good view of the lake. We took turns inhaling from another can of air duster I'd taken from the mansion, and tried to maintain a conversation while floating in and out of consciousness. I didn't know Brandon to be very interested in drugs, and we'd never done any together, but somehow this felt comfortably within the realm of things I could suggest we do.

"Clearlake is kind of pretty," I said. "I never realized it when I lived here."

"Yeah. It was much easier to focus on the petty bullshit," he said.

He inhaled from the can and was gone for ten seconds.

I took the can from his limp grip and took a hit. Consciousness momentarily left me, leaving nothing to interpret the sensory intake of my body. The world womp-womp-womped as my brain cells died.

"I don't know what I'm doing with my life. I need to get out of Clearlake," Brandon said.

I nodded and handed him the can of duster. He took a hit and his head fell back onto his headrest. He looked angelic to me, but I was losing brain cells at a rapid rate, so there is a good chance that what I was seeing was the beautiful effect of the world disintegrating around me.

"Whenever I do drugs," I said, "I feel like if I died I wouldn't care at all. Like I just accept the possibility of death and it doesn't scare me."

"Same," he said.

"Then when I'm not on drugs I get really sad and guilty about how I felt when I was on drugs."

"I can see that."

•

We went to a bonfire party in an abandoned dirt lot off a dirt road. Brandon didn't really want to go, but I pushed for it.

"What else are we going to do?" I said.

There were forty or fifty people standing around a massive open fire, including all of my least favorite people from high school. Several guys were wrestling near the flames. Some drunk girls with exposed midriffs squealed as another girl drank from a beer bong. A person I knew to be a crackhead put a limp wrist to his chest to indicate the word *retard*.

"I feel like we're aliens trying to make sense of some nonsensical civilization that is about to self-destruct," Brandon said.

"This party would be a good setting for a trashy coming-of-age story," I said.

We watched someone barf all over his own shirt, take off the shirt, and start drinking again. Someone else spit loogies into the fire while nodding and swaying to music that either we didn't hear or was nonexistent. Another person was slumped over into the dirt, as if it were the most natural time and place to take a nap.

"God, this town makes everyone so stupid and terrible," I said.

"It's not the town's fault," Brandon said. "These people were going to be stupid and terrible no matter where they grew up."

"I don't know."

I liked believing that the town had caused such stupidity, because it made me feel strong and intelligent for overcoming it, for making my life interesting despite the bullshit that surrounded me. I was like a beautiful and unlikely fungus growing out of an old, dried-out cow patty.

It was cold outside, but Brandon and I wandered away from the fire and stood in a far corner of the lot taking turns with the duster. Once in a while, some drunk person I vaguely recognized would stumble toward us to ask if we had any cigarettes or alcohol.

We stayed until the bonfire went out, all the beer cans were empty, and mostly everyone had left.

I had felt a deep, all-encompassing apathy for most of the night. I had a complete lack of interest in people or my own feelings or what time it was or the reality of death. It felt like the deepest depression I had ever known but without all the exhausting emotions. It was a feeling that felt like the answer to all the problems of the world.

"What should we do now?" I said.

"I heard some people say they were going to DJ's house to hang out," Brandon said. "We could go over there."

We went to DJ's, but I don't think either of us knew why. The can of duster was still pretty full, but I was starting to get a headache. I drank from a vodka bottle. Brandon picked up an acoustic guitar that was lying on the carpet in the corner of the room and started playing.

"That's my guitar, but you can play it, I don't care," someone said. He introduced himself as Lyle. He had long black hair streaked with purple, three eyebrow rings, and eye makeup smeared across his cheeks, possibly from crying. I guessed he was fifteen or sixteen.

"Oh, cool, are you sure?" Brandon said. "I assumed it was DJ's guitar."

"Yeah, man."

Lyle sat down and listed all the different types of alcohol he had consumed in the last twelve hours. Shots of vodka. Beer. Shots of Hot Damn. Peppermint Schnapps with juice. More beer. More shots of vodka.

"That's a lot," I said.

"Eh," he said. "I like to drink as many different things as I can so I can black out and not remember throwing up."

I was drawn to Lyle's strange beauty. He looked like the son of two gorgeous, closely related fashion models. His eyes were huge and dark and too far apart. His whole body seemed delicate and limp, as if he hadn't ever considered the option of becoming strong. He seemed sad and pathetic in an iconic way.

The way I looked at him was the way I wanted others to look at me. I wanted to love and protect him. I handed him my can of duster and instructed him to inhale as he pressed down on the nozzle. He did so without hesitation.

"Don't do that shit, dude," someone said, glaring at me as if I were an unknown out-of-town adult giving toxic fumes to a probably troubled teenager. "That is really fucked-up and stupid."

The person speaking, who looked fifteen or sixteen, picked Lyle up by the wrist and led him to the kitchen, where a group of people were shotgunning beers.

I felt embarrassed. What was I doing? And why was I here? Not just here at this house. Why was I in Clearlake at all? If I hated it so much, why was I here? Why had I spent the whole night following people around who I claimed not to like, noting all the things I didn't like about them and adding those things to my massive list of reasons I had left Clearlake in the first place?

I was not a beautiful, magical fungus. I was part of the shit. I hadn't come back to observe the shit stains of my youth with ironic distance; I'd come back so I could act shitty and stupid while still feeling superior. I had come here so I wouldn't feel accountable for my own behavior.

Brandon dropped me off at my mom's rental mansion and we said our goodbye-don't-know-when-we'll-see-each-other-agains. Whether I would ever return to Clearlake, and if Brandon would be here when I did, were always indeterminable whenever we parted ways. If things went well for us, we likely wouldn't be in Clearlake at the same time, and we'd probably never see each other again. It was hard not to hope for it.

I lay down in the home theater room that was my bedroom for the weekend. Thick red velvet curtains were pulled back on each side of the giant TV screen. I unzipped my sleeping bag and got up to see if the curtains could actually be untied, or if they were permanently drawn, a pointless adornment merely to underline the fact that this was a "theater room," not just a room with a big TV in it, as I suspected was the case.

The curtains were sewn together in perfect pleats, and the tassels that appeared to be holding them loosely were just another decoration, also sewn in place, indicating that, yes, this was an elaborate facade designed to make other TVs seem lesser by comparison, even though, when it came down to it, TVs without curtains lacked nothing but the evident fear of their own inadequacy.

In the morning I stuffed another can of air duster and two spatulas into my backpack before going back to Oakland.

14

ROMANTIC COMEDY

I was just beginning to feel comfortable with the thought that I would be alone for the rest of my very lonely life when I realized I was in love with my friend Ian.

Ian, who had been my friend for three years. Ian, who I had worked with in our school's Facilities Department the year before and who had made it his personal goal each day to let everyone on the team know what a useless and lazy employee I was. Ian, who sang to himself during class worktime despite it being the most annoying thing any person could ever do. Ian, who once bragged that everything he was wearing he'd found on the street. *Wait. Ian?*

I was surprised by my own feelings, which were sudden and strong, just as it always is in romantic comedies when the girl realizes the guy she's been looking for has been there all along. But in romantic comedies they don't communicate to you how confusing that is, or how uncomfortable it is to start thinking of your friend in this new, perverted way, or how awkward you feel when you have to talk to that person for the first time after your feelings have been revealed to you. What do you say, exactly? Do you reintroduce yourself? Do you take your glasses off and whip your hair around dramatically so he finally sees you as a woman?

"Thai iced tea," I decided to say, the best and only way, I thought, to let him know that I was both available and interested. "Very nice choice."

"Get your own," he said, and walked away from me.

I followed him out of the campus café and to the cement retaining wall that students used as a bench, the one Ian had criticized me for repainting too slowly during our time together in Facilities. He adjusted something in his bag and then got up and walked away again.

"Where are you going?" I said.

"The painting studio," he said.

"Okay, I'll come with you. I have an hour before my class starts."

I walked beside but slightly behind Ian to the painting studio, where he sat at a table, opened a textbook, and started reading.

"What are you doing?" I said.

"Reading an essay about Man Ray for class."

"That's cool," I said.

I stood there for a minute, knowing I was going to leave but not wanting to leave too abruptly, which might indicate that something was wrong, and then, after what seemed like a normal amount of time to stand looking at someone reading, I left.

I compiled a list of the things I liked about Ian, as if I were collecting evidence.

He was smart and was always prepared for class and read books for pleasure. He was weird, even for art school. But he wasn't ironic or self-deprecating for the sake of being ironic or self-deprecating, and didn't have any of the pointless, self-conscious affectations that people develop to be seen as cool. He didn't seem embarrassed about himself. He was cute and manly and tall. He had beautiful and interesting hands. He was funny and laughed easily and had a way of making people feel comfortable. He held me accountable for having a poor work ethic at Facilities.

But I hadn't wanted to be held accountable, I reminded myself. It was a dumb work-study job that nobody took seriously except for him. I hated him that summer.

Then why had I put it on my list of his positive traits? Did I secretly relish being told I wasn't putting forth the effort I could have? That putting effort into menial work reinforces the drive to put effort into the work you care about? Did I subconsciously interpret his criticism as a sign that he cared about me and wanted me to do well in all aspects of my life?

I looked over my list carefully, to see if I had been fully honest. Everything checked out.

It was official, I conceded. I was in love with Ian. I ripped the list up into hundreds of pieces and placed the pieces in different trash cans around the apartment so they could never be placed together again.

I had been living with William for three years, and I normally told him everything, especially the things that most made me look sad and pathetic. Being sad and pathetic was something I had grown to be very good at, and William helped me cultivate being sad and pathetic into something I found funny and worthwhile, but for some reason I couldn't tell him that I was in love with Ian. I didn't want to be taken for sad and pathetic in this instance, when I felt that those words applied to me more perfectly than ever before.

It had been so long since I had romantically pursued anyone that I had no idea what to do. I decided to call Ian on the phone, which was something I rarely inflicted on people. I would ask him to hang out, and then, when he realized that I meant hang out *just the two of us*, he would realize I had feelings for him. It was bold, it was assertive, and it was direct. Not as bold, assertive, and direct as telling him what my feelings were, but a very close second.

"Hey, what's up?" he said.

"Oh, nothing. I was just seeing what you were doing and if you wanted to hang out."

"I'm on a bus to Los Angeles for the weekend. One of my classes is going to a show there, but I'm going early to hang out with some family who lives nearby."

"Oh. Okay."

"How is your senior project coming along?"

We talked for twenty minutes, as if there were nothing unusual about the two of us talking on the phone together. The call was suddenly dropped and I took the phone away from my ear and stared at it, unsure of what to do. Ian texted me ten minutes later, saying that his bus had gone through a tunnel and his phone dropped the call, and that he would see me next week.

William was consumed with finishing art for his senior show, as were most of my friends. As an Individualized Major, I was not officially part of any department, so department graduation requirements didn't apply to me. I had finished the Writing Department's fifty-page thesis requirement months before (voluntarily), and had performed a reading early in the semester for my senior show (also not technically required of me), so for the rest of the year I spent most of my time alone in my bedroom, writing for pleasure while waiting to graduate.

It was odd, waiting for graduation. I wanted it to come quickly, so that my friends would not be stressed out and busy anymore, so that we could all start the careers and easy, art-filled lives we thought would present themselves to us. But I also wanted the end of school to never come. I was afraid of the responsibility of deciding what my life would be, and didn't want to face the future I'd set up for myself.

•

On a gloomy Monday after ten hours of studio time on campus, I found a plastic flower stuck between the brake cables of my bike. I always parked my bike on a side street away from campus where other bikes were rarely parked. I picked up the flower. It was dirty and looked like it had been run over.

Who would do this? A secret admirer? Ian? Maybe it was a random act of kindness performed by a stranger walking by. Maybe it was Ian.

I tried to put Ian out of my mind. I recognized this kind of thought process. These were the kinds of thoughts that would quickly lead to an unhealthy obsession, which would make it impossible to see Ian clearly, which would pollute my relationship with him before the relationship even had a chance to occur.

This is just what would happen in a romantic comedy, I thought. So does that make it less likely that Ian is responsible for the plastic flower, because real life is never like the movies? Or does it make it more likely, because life imitates art, and just the fact that I'm comparing my life to romantic comedies makes it more likely that I would unconsciously fabricate a situation like this for myself?

I began to find small toys or colorful garbage stuck between my brake cables or wrapped around my handlebars a few times a week. This wasn't my imagination running away with itself. This wasn't happening to other bikes in the area. I was being singled out by someone who knew that I liked tiny useless things.

"I found this on my bike," I said to William, showing him the toy deer whose legs had fit perfectly around my handlebars, being as nonchalant as possible so as to not embarrass myself if it turned out that William had been responsible for the toys the whole time.

"Oh, weird," he said.

"Are you doing this?" I said. "I find things on my bike all the time."

"No. Oh my god, I would never think to do something like that."

•

Ian was in a band called Shannon and the Clams with our other friends Cody and Shannon. I started going to all their shows. It was the easiest and most natural way to be around Ian without it seeming obvious that I was interested in him. As the drummer, Ian was always the most preoccupied with setting up and breaking down and watching over band equipment, so he wasn't always available to hang out before or after they played.

"Cool show," I'd usually manage to say.

"Thanks for coming out," he'd say.

"I love you," I said one night. I was very drunk, and Ian was trying to pick me up off the ground.

"I really do," I said, unintentionally falling into his body.

"I love you, too," he said, and laughed.

"Last night when I was really drunk, I told Ian I loved him," I later told William. It was my first attempt to tell William I had a crush on Ian.

"Wow, that's really embarrassing."

"I'm going to become the kind of drunk person who tells everyone I love them."

"No, you shouldn't do that anymore," William said.

"I can't control myself when I'm drunk."

"Oh, you can, too," he said.

I was pathetic, but that was a fact I had accepted years before, that I had moved past, that then slowly had begun to bother me again, which I talked about with my closest friends in a tone that implied I was actually too self-aware to be pathetic, that I then explored through writing, and finally fully embraced. I was pathetic! It opened me up to carrying out all kinds of inadvisable but exciting behavior, like telling the person I loved that I loved him while very drunk.

"You're not going to like this," William said, "but I think I'm going to move back to South Dakota after school ends."

"Finally, no more roommate drama," I said sarcastically. We'd had one serious fight in the three years we lived together. There was never any drama between us. However, we had shared our apartment with a rotating cast of third roommates, who we never put our minds to liking and therefore never got along with, always passive-aggressively pushing them into other living situations within a year. We seemed to only be able to live with each other.

"Who am I going to live with?" I said.

"You're going to have to figure that out."

"I don't know how to be a person without you."

The opening for Ian's senior show was on the San Francisco campus of our college at a time when I would already be there for class. He was presenting a series of large layered polymer cutouts in reds and flesh tones splattered with gray and blue. Some of them resembled internal organs, and some resembled mutants whose faces resembled a vagina and whose entrails seemed to be escaping from their necks. I looked at the pieces briefly during a class break, and then more carefully after class. I had not seen much of Ian's art before this show. I had seen him working in his studio, when the cutouts were not pieced together yet and were just abstract shapes.

"What do you think?" Ian said.

"It's really gruesome and weird," I said.

"Too weird for you?"

"I'm not saying that."

I got the feeling we might not be talking about his art anymore, that our conversation had turned into a metaphor for our relationship.

"I thought you liked weird things."

"Sometimes. Usually," I said. "I like this show. I didn't know what to expect. Your treatment of the polymer is really beautiful."

I ate some of the crackers and cheese Ian had put out while he talked to other people. I realized that the shuttle back to Oakland, where we both lived, was leaving in ten minutes, but Ian didn't seem prepared to leave.

"Are you going back on the shuttle?" I asked.

"I think Cody is coming and I'll get a ride back with him."

"Oh, do you think I could get a ride too?" I wanted to keep hanging out. Now that school was almost over I didn't know if I would get to see him much, other than at his shows, where it was so hard to hang out with him.

"Probably."

"Do you think I should stay and find out?"

"I don't know. You can if you want."

Discouraged by Ian's lack of interest in my staying, I left and caught the shuttle back to Oakland.

"I want a dog really bad," I said. We were drinking whiskey in a crappy bar after one of his shows.

"Really?" Ian said. "You want a dog?"

"Yeah," I said. "Really bad."

I had the feeling, again, that we were not talking about what we were talking about. "The dog" was a relationship, and we were using this code to talk about our feelings for each other, my desire to be with him, and his understanding of my feelings.

"What would you do with a dog?" he said.

Embarrassed to be talking about our relationship so plainly, I tried to confuse things so I couldn't be held responsible for what I was or wasn't saying.

"Neglect it," I said.

The only thing standing between me and Ian was a lifetime of convincing myself that I didn't want the things I wanted most.

This is much better than a relationship, I would tell myself, gesturing to the debris around my bedroom: books half read and abandoned in the crevice between my bed and the wall, laundry that was neither clean nor dirty, the coffee cup I had used for a month without washing, a large box of expired condoms that were of no use to me but that I had carried from my last apartment to this one hoping they would start to mean something to me artistically. *Because this is real life. Life is a constant longing for something else. Longing is superior to love, and is also superior to pain, the inevitable feeling that would come from the inevitable rejection if my feelings about Ian became clear to him.*

"William is moving out at the end of the semester," I said, "in case you're looking for a new apartment."

"I do have to move out of my apartment," Ian said. He looked at me suspiciously, the way someone might look at a toddler who has just lied about pooping her pants.

"I don't think it would be a good idea," he said.

"Why? You don't like me?"

"No, it's not that. I just wouldn't want to risk ruining our friendship."

"Please don't move," I said to William. "Just continue living with me until we're old and miserable."

"I wish I could," he said.

"So don't go. I'll help you unpack. I'll tell our landlord we are staying after all."

"Okay. Can you also get someone to pay my rent and buy me food and art supplies?"

"Yes."

Without William, I would be just one free-floating person, attached to nothing and nobody. Without William or school, why stay in Oakland? What did I have there anymore? But then why move anywhere else? Where else in the world was there anything for me?

"Don't be so dramatic," William said. "It's not like I'm going to live in South Dakota forever."

"I know," I said.

But I didn't know anything.

One day, very close to the end of the semester, instead of a toy or flower, I found a note on my bike.

"I want to meet U yes I'm lonly," it read. It was written in thick black marker in strange, alien-like handwriting on the back of a Safeway receipt for the purchase of a mini carton of milk and an unidentified bakery item made earlier that same day.

I want to meet U. I turned the phrase over in my head, trying to glean alternative meaning. Did someone want to meet me based on the appearance of my bike? Or was it someone who had seen me with my bike? *Yes I'm lonly.* So did this person want to meet me *because* they were lonely? That didn't seem like a very promising introduction.

The handwriting was odd. At first I interpreted it as contrived to intentionally disguise itself, but now, looking closer at it, it seemed familiar.

I biked home quickly and opened my box of treasured belongings to find the letter Ian had sent me the year before when he was studying abroad in Sweden.

The extra loop in the *a* was a perfect match to any of the numerous *a*'s in his letter. The airiness of the *w*'s were identical. The whole note had the appearance of having been written backwards and upside-down. The pressure of the penmanship seemed to match.

It was Ian's handwriting for sure.

"Did you enjoy your milk and bakery item today?" I texted.

"What," Ian texted back.

"You wrote your note on the back of a receipt."

"Oh yeah. Did you like it?"

"Yes."

"I spelled a word wrong, though."

"No, you didn't."

"Yeah, I did. The word *lonely* is supposed to have an 'e.'"

"You can drop the 'e' if you want."

"No, it's supposed to have an 'e.'"

I didn't see Ian again until graduation. I approached him, initiated a hug, congratulated him on his achievement, accepted congratulations for my own achievement, and then we stood awkwardly among our peers.

"Are your parents here?" I said.

"Yeah," Ian said. "Want to meet them?"

"Yeah, actually I do," I said. "I have something important to ask them."

I was joking, but Ian called over his parents who were a few feet away, introduced us, and told them I wanted to ask them a question.

"Oh no, I don't have a question," I said, and excused myself, explaining that I desperately needed water before the ceremony started.

After the ceremony I texted Ian asking if he was going to the party that a lot of our friends were going to.

"The band has a show tonight," he said. "But maybe we will all come to the party afterwards."

My cousin Alana had come to see me graduate, and since she was underage we couldn't go to the show. I took her to the party and texted Ian several times from there, and he kept replying that maybe they would come, but they never did, and I didn't talk to him again until his next show.

Despite Ian's having seemingly admitted his feelings for me in the note, and my addressing those feelings by text, nothing changed between us. He didn't text me more frequently or with any sense of urgency. He neither approached me nor avoided me at his shows, but treated me like the friend I had been for five years, who he would probably talk to at some point in the night but who was not an immediate priority.

I resigned myself to the fact that I was not the protagonist in a romantic comedy. There was no romantic comedy. Any sign that indicated to me that there might have been was a sad fabrication. I was wrong about what the note had meant.

The day after graduation, William and I climbed out of his bedroom window and onto our roof. It was a mildly warm summer day in Oakland. One could choose to wear denim jeans and a light sweater or tiny shorts and a tank top and feel comfortable either way. We drank daiquiris and talked about nothing, looked out on our scenic view of a few parked cars, the corner of a liquor store, and thick blooming vines growing around a trellis.

William was moving away in a couple of weeks, but for now we sipped our drinks and said these positive, meaningless things to each other, avoiding all the difficult questions of direction and money and purpose.

"Are you going to miss Oakland?" I said.

"Ew, not at all," he said.

I wasn't very upset the day William left, because, the night before, we had gotten into an argument about who would get to use the vacuum first as we finished cleaning our apartment.

He climbed into the U-Haul that was parked in our driveway, and I could tell he was still thinking about the vacuum, which was now packed up with all his other things in the truck. My things were packed in boxes too, still in our apartment, ready to move into my new place later that day.

It's his vacuum, I thought, not knowing whether that fact strengthened his case for being able to use the vacuum whenever he wanted, or my case for being able to use it freely the last night before it was taken from me, maybe forever. It was possible that I would never see the vacuum again. Neither of us could really promise anything, one way or the other.

"I miss you already," William said, his hands firmly gripping the steering wheel as he turned out of our driveway.

"It's not too late to change your mind," I said. "Or maybe I should come with you?"

"Chels," William said.

I never saw the vacuum again.

15

ZEITGEIST

Dean was a friend of a friend of a friend. I met him at a warehouse party in West Oakland that Stella Artois and Camel cigarettes were sponsoring. An unlimited supply of both was free to everyone there. Dean worked for Camel, and told me they were looking for people "like me" to join the team.

"Basically, we need people to go to bars around San Francisco and chat with people and give them free packs of cigarettes and get them to sign up for our newsletter," he said.

It sounded like something I would be terrible at that would also challenge my ethics, but I needed employment badly. When college ended two weeks earlier, my work-study jobs had ended as well. I was quickly running out of money. I agreed to meet up with him later in the week to hear more about the position.

We met at Zeitgeist, a hipster bar in San Francisco, in the early afternoon. Dean bought me a beer and we sat at a table outside with some friends of his who were also there. I listened to them talk about DJ equipment and types of facial piercings. Every once in a while Dean would compliment my appearance, or ask me if I thought something he just said was funny. I awkwardly sipped my beer and considered if I could extract myself from this "interview" before it had technically begun.

"I'm not sure if you're right for this position," he finally said. "But my friend Crystal is hiring an assistant to work at her salon. We could go talk to her if you want. It's really close to here."

"Sure," I said.

We left Zeitgeist and wandered around San Francisco in a seemingly aimless way. I had asked where the salon was before we left the bar, but I didn't recognize the street name, so I had no idea where we were going. As we walked, I began to feel very drunk and scared, but I tried to keep myself poised as if I were in an interview. He talked to me about parties and the San Francisco club scene, and I nodded politely and sometimes said, "Mmhmm," or "Whoa, cool."

San Francisco is a small city, but I have always had a poor sense of space and direction, so I was completely lost pretty much from the moment we left Zeitgeist.

Dean took me into another bar and ordered us drinks. I sipped mine very slowly, not really wanting to drink anymore but appreciating the social crutch of having something to do with my hands and mouth.

"We should write a book together," Dean said.

"Uh-huh."

"I'm a pretty talented illustrator. You'd be really impressed."

"Cool."

I looked at the people playing pool a few feet away, embarrassed that they might be overhearing the conversation I was in. Dean called over the bartender and ordered more drinks.

He leaned over the table and kissed me on the mouth. I smiled uncomfortably, feeling disgusted with him, but not wanting him to see that feeling on my face, not wanting him to feel bad, not wanting to make things awkward.

"You're so cute," he said.

I was drunk in that way where nothing made sense, and I kept thinking, *This probably makes sense but I'm too drunk to put it together.* I wanted to go home, to stop hanging out with Dean, to never see him again, but I also wanted to appear appreciative and eager to please. I couldn't shake my stiff, pleasant, agreeable interview personality.

I wanted to buy a hot dog from the hot dog cart outside the bar, but couldn't bear to part with the four dollars. It wasn't that four dollars was out of my budget for a meal, exactly, but I had already spent four dollars on the BART ride from Oakland, and would spend another four dollars riding it back whenever this miserable job interview or date or whatever ended. I had food waiting for me at home, and I couldn't afford to have a twelve-dollar day.

This wouldn't be the last time I would unintentionally end up on a date while trying to interview for a job. A few years after this, I would apply for a personal assistant position and, on what I thought was a second interview, see the remake of *Fame* in a theater and, later that night, politely turn down an invitation to the spa.

"Are you hungry?" Dean said.

"Yes, so hungry," I said. I hoped Dean had psychically heard my wishes for a hot dog.

"I know of a cute little sushi place down the block," he said. "Let's go there."

I realized, as we left, that I knew what bar we were in, and that I knew how to get to the BART station from where we were. After the sushi place, I thought, would be a perfect time to leave. I would say, *Well, it's been great, let me know about the salon, I guess*, and then head toward the train.

I ordered a side of edamame and let Dean order the actual food, so that there would be no confusion about who was paying. He ordered appetizers, big plates of sashimi, and hot sake, with which we cheers'd several times for various things he had talked about during the day.

When the bill came, Dean said he didn't have any more money on his card, and that if I paid for the meal he could get me cash from his apartment a few blocks away. The bill was $150, exactly half of all the money I had in the entire world.

This is one of those times in my life when I wish I could go back and hug myself. I was drunk, yes, and scared of what would happen if we left without paying, yes, but, more than that, I really thought I might still have a chance at one of these (in retrospect, clearly nonexistent) jobs, and I was desperate for employment. I didn't want to ruin my chances by being petty and afraid.

I paid the bill and followed him to his apartment. On the way, I texted my friends Ian and Cody. I knew they were playing a show on this side of the Bay later that night. I casually asked them where and when the show was, not wanting to reveal the situation I was in, then immediately changed my mind and texted, "I'm going to this guy's house near the Mission and I'm afraid." I hoped they would understand the complexities of the situation from that one text.

"Where are you?" Cody texted.

"We are setting up in Haight, want us to pick you up when we're done?" Ian texted.

"Yes," I texted Ian, trying to conceal my phone from Dean.

"I'll need an address," he texted.

We arrived at the apartment.

"I'll just wait out here," I said. I couldn't see an address anywhere, and wanted to walk to the end of the block to see the street signs.

"It's cold out here. Don't be crazy," Dean said.

"I'm fine," I said. "It's not cold at all."

"Just come inside. It will just take a minute," he said.

"That's fine, then just go grab the money and bring it to me."

"Come on, don't make me feel stupid," he said.

I followed him into his apartment, not wanting him to feel stupid, preferring, for some reason, to take the feeling of stupidity that was quickly expanding inside me and enlarge it even further to accommodate this stranger's baseless request that I not make him feel stupid.

His apartment was large and dark, with trendy furniture and dirty clothes laid all over everything. He didn't turn on any lights, and excused himself to the bathroom. I stood in the center of the room, not wanting to sit on his bed, which was the only available seat.

"I don't have an address," I texted Ian and Cody. "Can you come to the Mission and I'll find you?"

Dean came out of the bathroom and pulled out two $100 bills from a dresser drawer. I immediately felt relieved. The screaming voice in my head that told me I was about to be raped had been wrong. Here was the money to prove it.

"Here's your money," he said, throwing the money onto the bed. "But if you take it, you can forget about getting a job."

I made an earnest effort to understand what he was saying, trying to figure out why one determined the other. I also did some quick math and realized that if I took the money, it would not only pay for the meal but also my BART rides, plus something like forty dollars extra. It was forty dollars versus a job where I would possibly have to interact with Dean again.

I picked up the money.

Dean grabbed me from behind and pushed me onto the bed. He took the money from my hand and threw it onto the floor, then softly kissed my neck.

"Don't be stupid, Chelsea," he said.

I briefly considered allowing myself to be raped. It had been such a long day. I was drunk and felt physically weak, and didn't know what to do to get myself out of this situation. I had made a number of mistakes that led me to this place with this person. I had been quiet when I should have spoken up. I had been afraid to be too forward and so had failed to keep the conversation pointed to employment. I had entered his apartment when I knew I shouldn't. I had ignored red flags and allowed myself to be dragged around the city by someone I didn't trust. Had this all really been for a job?

I had a flashback of myself from that morning, making a balanced breakfast and putting on my finest interview attire. I thought I was going to get a job, a real job, with a commute and a dissociation from my personal values. I had felt so proud of myself, so strong and ready to take control of my life. What a contrast to the pathetic, voiceless person I was now, mere hours later, failing to even attempt to prevent myself from being raped.

"I have to go to the bathroom," I said. I said it weakly, expecting to be pushed back onto the bed. But he let me up, and I ran out of his apartment and into the street. I texted Ian and Cody as I walked back in the direction we had come. "When do you think you'll come over here?" I wrote. Then Dean was behind me, pushing me into a taxi.

He directed the taxi driver to an address, and I typed what he said into my phone and sent it to Ian and Cody.

"They just called me," Dean said. "We're gonna go down to the office and have you fill out an application for the Camel Spokesperson job."

"Okay," I said. I didn't believe him, and hoped that Ian and Cody would beat us to wherever we were actually going, that I could jump from the taxi into the arms of people I trusted.

We arrived at a giant warehouse. I looked at the dark nondescript street that seemed more like an alley, wondering if I would be able to find the BART station if Cody and Ian didn't come through.

We went inside and he gave me a Stella Artois and a job application clipped onto a clipboard. There was another guy there, and Dean introduced me as the newest member of the team.

"We're almost there," Cody texted.

I began filling out the application with fake information, simultaneously looking obsessively at my phone.

"You'll have to interview with my boss," Dean said. "But he's a great guy, really super chill."

"Okay," I said. I had no intention of meeting with anyone or ever talking to Dean again, but I didn't want to piss him off before I escaped.

"It's not an interview so much as a meet and greet. I'm the one who decides if we're going to hire you or not."

"Oh, cool," I said.

"We're here," Cody texted.

I got up and walked out of the warehouse. Dean followed me, and I ran towards Cody's van, which was right outside.

"What the fuck," Dean yelled as I got in the van. "You stupid bitch. You'll never get a job, you dumb slut."

He chased us down the alley like in a horror film, and I sunk deep into my seat, filled with shame and thankfulness and disbelief.

Ian turned around in the passenger's seat to look at me. He was wearing the red checkered shirt that was his band costume, and seemed full of energy, clearly ready to play a show and party. I smiled at him.

Thank you, I thought.

"Who was that guy?" he asked.

I shook my head, afraid that if I thought about what had happened or almost happened I would start to cry.

They took me to the show they were playing that night, and I hugged everyone I recognized well over the socially agreed-upon hugging duration. When the band started playing, I sat by myself on a couch in the back of the room, watching the audience dance and laugh.

16

EVOLUTION AND MAYBE DEATH

"Would it be all right if I stay at your apartment for a few days?" Jeppe wrote to me in an email.

I had met him in a bar in San Francisco after a poetry reading. He was my friend Josh's friend Marie's old classmate from Denmark. Jeppe and Marie were separately traveling around North America, as was apparently custom for Danes in their early twenties.

I was immediately entranced by Jeppe. He showed me the journals he was keeping, which were filled with funny observations and cute little drawings of things he had seen, mostly in Mexico so far. He had been reading a lot of Richard Dawkins, and we talked about *The Selfish Gene*. Everything he said was either funny or smart or both, and he paid equal attention to everyone who was part of the conversation.

"Of course you can stay with me," I wrote back. "I would love that."

I was living with three girls, including Shannon, who shared a bedroom with me. Shannon consistently let the touring bands she played with sleep over, and one of our other roommates once dragged my mattress out of my room and into hers so she could have sex on it, so I figured inviting a foreign near-stranger to stay with us for a few days without asking anyone beforehand was within the realm of acceptable roommate behavior.

I set up a bed for Jeppe between my bed and my roommate Shannon's bed, making our room 90 percent bed.

All my roommates loved him. It was actually annoying how much everyone loved him. Everyone wanted attention from him, and he moved casually between all of us in equal but unmeasured quantities of time. He had absolutely no character flaws, as far as I could tell. He was fun and funny and nice to be around and smelled good. He had perfected the art of being a social human.

He didn't explore Oakland much, instead visiting me during almost every shift at the chocolate café where I worked. "A few days" turned into a week, which turned into two weeks, which turned into three.

We went grocery shopping together, rode bikes to get ice cream cones, hung out at bars with my coworkers, and spent hours illustrating each other's writing. We wrote a short story together about a never-ending eBay transaction between two oversensitive eBay users, both characters sure they were ripping off the other and wanting to make things fair and equal.

We did everything together except make out, which was, increasingly, all I wanted to do with him.

"I really like Ian," Jeppe said one day. We had gone to see Ian's band, Shannon and the Clams, play the night before. "I like all your friends, but I really like Ian," he said.

"Yeah," I said. "I love Ian."

"I love how he dresses," Jeppe said. "Like how he wore that neon vest the other night. And how he always has a pocketknife. It's so different from everyone else, but not in a way that he's trying to be different. He's very unique. Most people are trying too hard."

"Yeah."

It boggled my mind how much fun I could have with Jeppe, how attractive I found him, how easy it was to be around him, how much we had in common, and how I could still feel a sharp pang of longing whenever I heard Ian's name.

"You're great," I said to Jeppe. I was consciously overcompensating for my mixed-up feelings, but it sounded unconvincing.

"You, too," he said, and I wondered if he was thinking of the person he was actually in love with too, wherever in the world that person was.

Jeppe decided he should probably leave Oakland and continue his travels, so on his last night in town, we went to see Ian's band play again. We danced hard and hugged each other tight, not wanting the night to end. Everyone got very drunk and went for hamburgers afterward. I didn't buy a hamburger because both Jeppe and Ian offered to share theirs with me. I took alternating bites of each of their burgers. I mostly wanted to eat Jeppe's burger, because Ian had ordered his with mayonnaise and I hated mayonnaise, but I couldn't pass up the thrill of eating from two men's burgers at the same time.

Jeppe and I biked home while my roommates took the band's van, but somehow we made it back to the house first.

Drunk and anxious about Jeppe leaving my life forever, I hugged him in my dark living room, then kissed him.

"Now I don't want to leave tomorrow," he said.

"Don't leave!" I said. "Stay here with me forever!"

He smiled.

My roommates enthusiastically agreed to let him stay longer—everyone still couldn't get enough Jeppe—but Shannon said he would have to start sleeping in my bed with me instead of a mattress on our bedroom floor. Which was fine, because now we were, like, together, or something.

We had sex the next night, and I found out that Jeppe actually did have a character flaw: sexual urgency.

"I like touching your body," Jeppe said. It was one of those very hot summer days that makes you feel like time stopped mattering a long time ago and you're just now realizing how little it ever really meant. We were lying on my bed, both facing the window.

"I like it too," I said.

"You like me touching your body?"

"Yeah."

"It seems like the perfect body. But it's not. Nothing's perfect."

I turned to face him, trying to will myself to feel either upset that he thought my body was less than perfect or flattered because he thought my body was close to perfect. I felt neither.

Jeppe actually had the perfect body. Like a mannequin. And the perfect personality, just the right ratios of humor, seriousness, intellect, and compassion. And great hair and teeth and skin. A nice laugh and charming mannerisms and a pleasant way of being. I looked at him the way I looked at a reproduction of a painting by Michelangelo or a large, exquisite rose garden. He was so wonderful that he became an abstraction. His features seemed more like representations of features than features themselves.

"Is this dating?" Jeppe said. "I don't understand American rules of dating. Is this it?"

"I guess so. I feel kind of detached because I know you're going to go back to Denmark soon."

"Like detached arms and legs?" he said, referring to something I had written in a poem that had struck a chord with him for some reason and that he kept bringing up.

"Um, I guess, in that that is a correct usage of the word *detached*."

"I don't want you to feel detached."

"I feel happy," I said. I smiled.

I felt really detached. I felt as if I were experiencing the memory of a relationship after it had already been over for years. I wasn't putting myself through any of the difficult aspects of being with somebody because I knew how and approximately when it would end. I didn't have to figure out how to best communicate with him, or to bother with jealousy, or worry about whether we were enough or right for each other. We had a simple, pleasant relationship, one that didn't require any of my heart.

"What do you believe in?" I said.

"Evolution. Maybe death. I think I believe in death," Jeppe said.

"Like you just die and disappear and then nothing?"

"Yes. You just die and that's it."

"Me too," I said.

I invited Ian over to hang out with me and Jeppe. I was feeling confident because I was with Jeppe, and therefore there could be no weirdness or ambiguity between me and Ian. Ian came over and the three of us sat in my living room, drinking beers.

"I'm never having kids," I said. It wasn't something I felt strongly about, but I was just seeing how it felt to say it.

"Don't want to ruin your beautiful vagina?" Ian said.

I let the word *vagina* sit in the air for a few seconds to let it enjoy its moment as the topic of conversation.

"I once had a doctor tell me I have a beautiful cervix," I said.

"I always think about that, how your doctor said you have a beautiful vagina," Ian said.

"I don't remember ever telling you that story," I said. "Also, my doctor said I have a beautiful *cervix*, not vagina."

"Oh," Ian said.

Ian doesn't know the difference between a cervix and a vagina, I thought.

"No one has ever said my vagina was beautiful," I said.

Jeppe excused himself to the bathroom and Ian said, "Why did you invite me here tonight?"

"I don't know," I said. "I just haven't seen you in a while."

"Oh," he said. "I got your text message and I was like, *Oh wow!* But I guess you always project your own desires."

"Yeah, well," I said.

After two months of living with me, Jeppe decided it was time to leave Oakland for real. He would travel to Portland and Seattle on his way to Vancouver, and he invited me to go with him for the first two cities.

We got a ride through Craigslist from a guy who drove a promotional energy drink truck. We stopped periodically at different cities along the way and helped him hand out energy drinks. The guy was like an energy drink personified, telling loud stories and laughing at his own jokes and finding all kinds of creative opportunities to exclaim, "Right on!" and "Right on, dude!"

I made Jeppe sit in the front seat. For the first time, he was annoying to me. His enthusiasm for helping out this weird energy drink guy seemed fake and excessive. Either that, or he was actually getting genuinely hyped from being around this guy, which was worse.

I began looking forward to the trip being over before we even made it to Portland. This trip seemed to be ruining the easiness and casualness of our relationship. Knowing that my time with Jeppe was coming to an end made everything seem more serious, and I couldn't enjoy being around him.

My friend Cody had set me up with his dentist friend in Portland, who offered to give me a really good deal on a partial denture I needed replaced, so each day I got up early and commuted to the dentist by myself to do the necessary impressions and fittings. Jeppe didn't have a phone, so meeting up with him was an annoying process that involved deciding where exactly to meet in a city neither of us was familiar with, and then finding that spot and staying there until the other person arrived. I would always be annoyed and grumpy by the time we found each other, and Jeppe would be relaxed in his I'm-just-a-foreigner-on-a-months-long-vacation way, which annoyed me further.

On our final day, an hour before our bus to Seattle, Jeppe told me he wanted to stay in Portland longer.

"Well, my flight back to Oakland is from Seattle tomorrow," I said. "I have to go."

"I know," he said.

I felt bad. I felt that I had betrayed my annoyance somehow, and that he knew that I wanted to get leaving him over with.

"I think I'm going to stay in Portland for a few more days," he said again.

"Okay."

"Or what? What should I do?" he said. I could tell he wanted me to beg him to come with me to Seattle, say something like *We only have one day left together*, and tell him how much I'd grown to love him.

"You should do whatever you want to do," I said.

"Tell me what to do."

"I can't."

"Maybe I'll stay in Portland."

"All right."

We walked around until my bus's departure time. We made shallow little observations about the scenery, and how beautiful Portland was, and how great their public transportation was.

"What are you going to do without me?" I said when we were nearing the bus station again.

"Replace you. You're the replaceable kind."

"You're lucky."

"No, just kidding. Whenever I say goodbye to someone I think that I'll never find anyone like her. And I never do. But I always find someone else."

•

"What will happen with you and Jeppe?" Ian said. I was back in Oakland, and had asked him to walk around Lake Merritt and drink forties with me.

"Well," I said, "I'll probably never see him again."

"Are you sad?"

"Not really," I said. "Not right now. We didn't have a great time in Portland. I kind of wish I hadn't gone. It seemed like just a little too much."

It felt good to be hanging out alone with Ian. I wasn't trying to read into his every word, looking for secret messages about his feelings about me. I liked him and I was enjoying his company. Maybe it didn't need to be a big deal.

"I didn't think he was that great," Ian said.

"Why?"

"It was very transparent the ways he'd try to impress you. Like that song he sang about you in that video you showed me."

"I liked that song," I said.

"Of course you did. Because it was flattery."

"Yeah. I was flattered. I don't know. I didn't think of it that way. It seemed genuine. He was really, genuinely charming."

"Yeah," Ian said. "He was very charming."

Ian looked at his phone and then showed me a text that said, "I know why you didn't come out tonight and it's lame."

"Who sent that?"

"Shannon," Ian said. "She wanted me to go to some show she and Cody were seeing tonight. She thinks I need to do more extracurricular stuff with the band. But it shouldn't upset her that I want to hang out with you."

I knew that Shannon knew I had a crush on Ian, because she had been making meaningful eye contact with me whenever Ian was brought up, and when I asked our roommate Laurel, who I had confided in about my crush, if she had told Shannon, Laurel just said, "What kind of meaningful eye contact? When?" and never answered my question.

"Yeah, I don't know why she would be upset."

"She sometimes has trouble when people don't want to hang out with her all the time. She knows I like you. I've talked to her about it."

She knows he likes me? I thought. *Like, likes-me-likes-me?* I was embarrassed of my brain for thinking the phrase *likes-me-likes-me.* Was this his way of telling me that he liked me? Or was I just misunderstanding his way of talking? Maybe he was saying it in a way I could misinterpret on purpose so that I would feel confused and my confusion would give him power somehow. Was I supposed to respond to that comment or were we still talking about Shannon?

"You're really confusing," I said.

"I feel like a pond without a square," he said after a long silence.

"A pond without a square," I said, trying to find meaning in his words.

"Pawn," he said.

"Oh. What?"

"Just like, I don't really know which way to move because things seem uncertain."

"Oh."

"Like I'm afraid to make moves."

"You're making some kind of move right now," I said. "Although I don't know what it is."

He drank the rest of his beer and left the bottle on top of a garbage bin for a homeless person to recycle. I saw that I still had half a beer left. I took one slow sip.

"You're very masculine in some ways," Ian said.

"Oh," I said.

"Just that you're very independent. Nothing else, really."

I felt helpless with my feelings.

•

The next day, Ian left to tour with the band for two weeks. It was almost a relief for him to be away, to put him out of my mind. I worked shifts at the chocolate café, went out to bars with my coworkers, and made dinner with my roommates. On my days off I wrote long prose poems about wanting things that were within reach yet never grabbing them, perfectly content and comforted by the fact that they were there within reach in case I ever decided to reach for them.

I talked to Ian on the phone once while he was gone, a few days before Halloween. I had been carving pumpkins the night before with some of my coworkers.

"Well, not carving," I said. "I was cleaning them out for other people to carve because I don't like carving them. But the spoon was hurting my hand so I started using my nails to scratch the pumpkin walls and my nails all separated from my nail beds because that was a bad idea."

"That's something I really like about you," Ian said. "Everything you choose to do you have this strong focus on it and you give it all your energy. It's very attractive."

"So now all my fingertips hurt, which is a really strange feeling," I said.

"Our relationship is really confusing," he said.

"Yeah, I'm confused by it, too."

"Ask me anything," he said. "I won't necessarily answer, but you can ask."

"No thanks," I said.

My roommates and I threw a big party at our apartment. It was a group birthday party for a couple of our friends, and a welcome home for the band, who were back from tour. We played music in the living room, and the party spilled into the kitchen, all the bedrooms, and into our long driveway.

As usual, I got very drunk very quickly, and started dancing with and sort of kissing a guy named Andrew who I had peed in front of in an alley the year before but who I otherwise never talked to.

At the end of a song, I left Andrew to see if there was any beer in our fridge. Ian was standing behind me when I closed the fridge. He asked me to follow him to our back porch, and I did.

We stood on the porch together, and I waited for Ian to say something. He led me to the porch, I thought, and it was his responsibility to guide this conversation.

Through the window of the kitchen door, we saw Andrew heading to the back porch.

"Here comes trouble," Ian said. He took my hand and led me down the back stairs and into the detached garage my roommates had converted into an art studio and called Spider World.

I hated Spider World because it was filled with spiders. I normally refused to go in there. It was damp and musty, with boxes of our landlord's old shit stacked precariously against the back wall, likely filled with spiders.

"Remember that time at your and William's first apartment, when Max and his two friends were over, and I was there making Rorschachs in your kitchen all night?" Ian said.

"Yeah," I said.

"Why was I doing that?"

"I don't know." I laughed.

"Why haven't we ever gone out, Chelsea?" Ian said.

"I don't know," I said.

"But you want to, eh?"

"I think you're really great."

"I like you because I like your brain," he said. "I like what you say."

"I like what you say too. I think you're one of the most emotional people I know."

"Really? I think of myself as being very cold and distant."

"I guess that's true."

"I think if we dated we would both change in ways that we liked," he said.

I hugged him, and he held me tight. He was a lot taller than I was, and my head sat centered on his chest. When I looked up at him he was looking down, and we kissed. We kissed for a couple of minutes, holding each other in dark, awful Spider World.

I was too drunk to fully appreciate the moment. It seemed like an experience separate from the reality of my life, something I wanted and anticipated but knew wasn't real, like a lucid dream.

Somebody opened the door, looked at us briefly, and then left.

"Do you want to take a walk?" Ian said.

We ran out of Spider World and onto the street. I wasn't sure what kind of walk we were taking, if it was a walk to the liquor store or a walk to a private alley to kiss more, and I didn't want to presume incorrectly so I waited for Ian to lead. Ian led us to his band's van that was parked a block away, and we sat in the backseat and kissed and held each other's hands.

I began feeling pangs of doubt. We were both drunk and this was not good. I didn't want to kiss Ian drunk, and I didn't want to be kissed by him drunk. Kissing drunk was something I did with people I didn't care about. Kissing drunk didn't prove that we liked each other. Even while we were still kissing, I began to feel rejected. I imagined his regret tomorrow, his worrying about how to tell me that he wasn't interested, that it was just a dumb, drunk mistake, that he hoped we could still be friends, that my friendship meant a lot to him.

"We should go back to the party," I said. I ran out of the van before him and back into my apartment.

Shannon stopped me at the front door and said, "Were you and Ian smooching?"

"No," I said.

"Yes, you were. I know that you were."

"We absolutely weren't."

"You just came from Spider World together and then went out front alone for a really long time. I'm not stupid."

"Well," I said. "Can we talk about it later?"

It was getting really late and I was really tired, but there were still a lot of people in my house. They were all drunk, and a lot of them were in my bedroom.

"We could go to Cody's," Ian said. "I'm going to sleep there tonight."

"Yeah," I said. It startled me that Ian was being so forward all of a sudden. I had taken his awkwardness and hesitance with me as symbolic of his real feelings and his fear about being rejected. Maybe I had misread him, or done something tonight that made him reevaluate his feelings for me. Maybe he wasn't interested in me seriously, but thought that since we were drunk and making out, we might as well sleep together.

"Do you want to go now?" he said.

"Maybe," I said. "I'm not sure. I don't know if that's a good idea."

"It's not like that. I just thought you were tired and weren't going to be able to sleep for a while if you stayed here."

"Okay. I think I'm just going to stay here anyway."

Ian rode his bike to Cody's, and I stayed up for hours while the partiers slowly left or passed out in various awkward spots around the apartment.

I tried not to think about Ian in the days that followed. I did my best to cherish the blissfully ignorant days between finally kissing Ian and inevitably finding out that his feelings for me were merely friendly. I tried to ignore my feelings of doubt and desperation, doing nothing to assuage or discourage them, just letting them lie in the back of my mind undisturbed. I was trying to cultivate a kind of dolce far niente, enjoying the sweetness of doing nothing, because moving in any direction would be too painful. I wanted to live forever in my state of ignorance. In fact, I wished that I had never kissed him, so that the possibility of kissing him remained in my future, something to work toward and look forward to.

Several days later, after not seeing him or talking to him at all, Ian called and said in a very serious tone of voice that we needed to talk.

I prepared myself to hear the worst. Ian realized what we did was a mistake. He was very drunk. We were both drunk. He sees me as a very good friend. He hopes things can be normal between us.

He came over and we rode our bikes to Lake Merritt. We bought forties at a liquor store and sat at the edge of the lake, barely talking.

"I want to ask you a question but I'm not sure how to phrase it," Ian finally said.

"Okay."

"Do you have an opinion about what happened on Friday night? Or, what is your opinion?"

"What are you asking me?" I said, refusing to be the first one to say what was going to be said, even if that meant it would never be said at all. "What do you want me to talk about?"

"I don't know."

We sat in silence for a minute, and I decided to try to be as straightforward as possible. It didn't benefit me to be anything but honest about my feelings for him. I liked him. I should just say, "I like you."

"It's complicated," I said. It wasn't at all complicated. I was lying. I was still trying to protect myself from becoming vulnerable by holding on to the last dying shreds of any doubt he might still hold about my feelings for him. What was the point?

"Actually," I said. "I feel good about it. I like you a whole bunch."

"Me too," he said. "I like myself a lot."

Minutes went by without either of us speaking. I counted five shooting stars. I tied my shoe. I peeled the label off my beer and polished the glass underneath it with my fingers.

"I think if we were in a relationship it would be very weird," Ian said, not looking at me.

"Why? Why wouldn't it be normal?"

"I just think it would be a very strange and unique relationship."

"I think it would be very intense," I said.

"I'm not into intense."

"Really?"

"Or, I don't know," he said. "Maybe I am."

17

I LOST A TOOTH AT WORK

I lost a tooth while eating pizza at work. "Lost," as in it fell out of my mouth and was nowhere to be found.

It was already a trying day. I was preparing Christmas merchandise for the chocolate café where I worked, and because the hand-packaged items were selling faster than I could package them, I was falling further and further behind.

My boyfriend Ian had come with pizza to cheer me up.

It was 9 p.m., and Ian and I were the only people in the warehouse. I was preparing to stay for several more hours to make sure there would be plenty of items available the next morning for everyone who needed a quick, moderately cute, sweet, edible gift for under twenty-five dollars.

"I think I swallowed my tooth," I said, feeling the outside of my throat with my fingers, as if the tooth might be poking out of it.

How long had my tooth been missing? I had no idea. I'd only noticed the tooth was gone because I periodically checked that I still had all my teeth by gliding my tongue across the front of them, and this time around they weren't all there.

The pizza was a large thin-crust with caramelized onions,

mozzarella, arugula, garlic, and lemon-thyme oil. The slices were pretty big. Did any of these details help me in this moment? No, not really. But my tooth had only been missing a few seconds. I was bound to have a thought of some practical use very soon.

It wasn't a real tooth. It was one of the two tooth-colored, tooth-shaped pieces of plastic that sat on either side of my top front teeth, and were attached to another piece of plastic, pink and semitranslucent, that was molded to fit against the roof of my mouth.

Okay, they were dentures. Though the specialized orthodontia term for it was *flipper.*

Flippers have a lifespan of less than one year, and are supposed to be used as a temporary fix for missing teeth. They are expensive to replace, and I didn't have dental insurance, so I tried to take care of them so they'd last as long as possible. This particular piece was the fifth I'd owned in eight years. I was supposed to take it out before I ate, because biting into food weakened the bond the fake teeth had with the pink plastic, but taking it out when it had recently been glued in with denture adhesive was likely to break it as well, so I tried to make the best choice about whether to take it out each time I ate. I'd made the wrong choice this time.

I took out what remained of my flipper and examined it. The tooth had cleanly snapped off from the thin pink plastic. I touched the other tooth. It felt firm.

I went to the bathroom, laid some brown paper towels in the sink, and ran water over them so they would stick to the sink, creating a cover for the drain. I performed each action calmly and methodically, as if I had been trained to handle this kind of emergency. I then began to try to make myself vomit.

I began with the traditional way to self-induce vomiting: sticking my fingers into my throat. It didn't work. I choked and gagged, but nothing came up. So I tried to physically force the recently eaten pizza out of my body by pressing into my abdomen with my fists and clenching my abs as tightly as I could.

I barfed into the sink and gently sorted through the barf with my fingers, searching for the missing tooth. It was chunky and hard to look through.

Vomit carefully, I told myself, *because there's a good chance the tooth could enter your nasal passages. And dig through the vomit pile even while you're vomiting. There's no sense in wasting any time.*

Also, try to keep your back straight. You have a posture problem. You're barfing, so don't worry about it right now. This is more like a general reminder. It could lead to serious issues down the line if you're not careful.

Speaking of which, weren't you supposed to be joining the gym? Or something? And was there something about trying to eat better? I guess you think pizza probably fits into that category, though.

Oh, and don't forget that your new showerhead is going to be delivered on Monday, so make sure you don't leave the house until it arrives. You're working on Tuesday and Wednesday, so if you miss it on Monday you'll have to call the post office to figure out how to pick it up. It will be a nightmare. Just make it your business to be home on Monday.

Or wait, maybe it's coming on Tuesday.

Ian stood behind me as I worked through the barf, looking horrified. I knew I was testing the limits of what I could do in front of him. As it was, we already had very few boundaries. We could burp, fart, pick zits, and pee in front of each other, no problem. We had barfed in front of each other when we were sick or drunk and it hadn't been a big deal, but we hadn't yet determined whether we could then dig through the barf with our fingers, looking for our own missing tooth in front of each other. It just hadn't come up.

My two missing teeth had been missing since I was around seven years old. My baby teeth fell out, and all my permanent teeth grew in except the two lateral incisors, which are easily the third and fourth most prominent teeth in your mouth, right after your top front teeth. I had evenly gappy teeth until I was fifteen, when I got braces to shove them all into their correct places. Once there was enough room, two fake teeth were attached to my braces, dangling there until my braces came off, when I got my flipper. The next step was dental implants, but my family had exhausted my dental plan with braces, and we had no money. Dental implants were expensive, and I was told I would have to wait.

If I had been more forward-thinking, I would have asked, "Wait for what? And for how long? Until I'm done with high school? When I'm in college? After college? In my thirties? When will dental implants ever be possible?" But I have never been very forward-thinking, and those questions didn't occur to me for a very long time.

I was sensitive about the subject because Clearlake had a big meth problem and a big poverty problem when I was growing up, and, unsurprisingly, many people couldn't afford dental work. Ask anyone in the region about Clearlake, and they'd inevitably make a joke about missing teeth. In Urban Dictionary, the definition for Clearlake, CA, is, "A place where no one has a full set of teeth." Someone in Clearlake once found a human skull in their yard, and the big joke was: *How are they going to identify the skull without dental records?* Har har.

I knew that the joke was directed toward meth heads who used until their teeth fell out, and wasn't meant for people with congenitally missing teeth like me. But I still felt insulted by the stereotype. I may not have been on meth, but I *did* live in Clearlake, I *did* have missing teeth, and I *was* too poor to fix them. I had done so much to separate myself from the stereotypes of my hometown. I'd left immediately after high school, put myself into debt to attend an expensive private art college, and now had a job catering to the high-end chocolate cravings of Oakland's most privileged stay-at-home mothers. But it only took a single second for my shame and embarrassment to come rushing back.

I was still the poor, toothless girl I had always been.

The tooth wasn't in the barf pile. I barfed again, but it wasn't in that barf, either. I barfed and barfed, until all the pizza had come up and all that was left was bile. The tooth was nowhere. I had swallowed it and my body was refusing to choke it up so that I would be reminded of my place in the world. Or, it was stuck in my nasal passages and the area around it would become infected and swollen and the mass would prevent nasal discharge from leaving my body and would build up inside my brain and slowly kill me.

I was exhausted. I lazily stirred the sink, hoping there was some chance I had missed it, not wanting to say goodbye to my tooth or my barf just yet.

"Here it is," Ian said. He was looking into the pizza box across the room.

I dragged myself over to the pizza box, knocking over my carefully stacked bags of homemade chocolate-covered marshmallows, and weakly examined the tooth, confirming that it was in fact my tooth and not some other stray pizza-box tooth.

At home, I glued the tooth back onto my flipper with regular super glue. The internet said it was barely toxic.

18

THE MAN WHO FAMOUSLY INSPIRED THIS ESSAY

I decided to stop having a dad one day in late winter when I was twenty-three.

Decided is too strong a word. It makes me sound confident and in control, and I was mostly frazzled and unsure.

A couple of months before this, the last time I had seen him, he'd picked me up in Oakland and we'd driven north together for Thanksgiving at the house my mom and Jett had recently moved into. During the hour-and-a-half car ride, my dad accused me of harboring resentment about him not being in my childhood, angrily asked why I didn't call him "Dad," told me that anything I heard about his supposed pill addiction was bullshit (I had not heard anything), told me I was being brainwashed by my mom and Jett, refused to listen to any counterargument regarding the brainwashing, told me I had a responsibility to visit L.A. to babysit his baby daughter, asked if I would consider going to group therapy with him, asked me not to call him "Dad" anymore because he didn't need that kind of pressure, and accused me of "faking" the bloody nose I got while crying in the dry heat of his car.

"You're going to thank me one day for giving you all of this material for your writing," he said when I stopped crying.

I avoided eye contact and silently promised to never write a damned thing about him.

My dad had a specific talent for saying things that made me hate things about myself that I had never considered problems before. Why wasn't I more enthusiastic and easygoing? Why didn't I color my hair? Why didn't I talk unprompted about my social life? Did I even have a social life? Why didn't I have a driver's license? Why had I never called my mom's husband "Dad"? Why was I so selfish and cruel as to not call my mom's husband "Dad"? Why did I wear my makeup like that? Did I think that looked good? Why wasn't I asking him questions about his life? Why wasn't I more curious about him? Was I completely socially inept? Or was I really just that self-centered?

I considered a visit with him successful if the depression it threw me into afterward lasted less than two weeks.

Before each visit, I told myself that this time would be different. I would be more lively and interesting, and tell him about all the things I liked, all the things that I liked about myself and were interesting to me. This time we would talk in a way that didn't feel forced and horrible. I would ask him emotional questions like, *What did you do after you left my mom? Did you ever think about me? Were you afraid to contact us?* And we would begin to feel the closeness I'd always assumed was the point of having a dad.

But when the time actually came to attempt these conversations, he would say something like "I don't want to talk about the past. I did what I had to do and I'm not going to be made to feel bad about it."

He wanted to start our relationship in the middle, without even addressing the fact that it had no beginning. To him, my anxiety and trepidation about our relationship were symptoms of resentment and anger that he decided I had before he even met me, when actually anxiety and trepidation were basic aspects of my personality that I brought with me into every situation. I felt fundamentally misunderstood.

"Why are you so fucking sad all the time?" he said to me once at the beach. I had just successfully stood upright on a surfboard while a baby wave slowly propelled it to the shore. I felt like I was beaming.

"I'm not sad," I said, trying to visualize my own face. Was I frowning?

"Jesus, you look like someone just died."

I internalized our lack of connection and blamed myself for it, which gave me an air of insecurity and weakness, traits my dad found pathetic, further snowballing our problems with each other.

I cried to my mom over the phone about how I broke one of my fake teeth and barfed up my dinner trying to find it, how expensive it would be to see the dentist with no insurance, and how it would take months to save up enough money just to replace my dumb little flipper. My mom talked to my nana, and then my nana called me to tell me the whole barfing thing wasn't going to happen again.

"It's going to be really expensive," I said. "The quote I got years ago was like six thousand dollars."

"Well, good," she said. "I'm an old lady and have nothing much to spend my money on, anyway."

I was hesitant to let my nana pay for such a thing, because money had caused problems in our family before, and because I didn't know how well my nana understood her own finances. But she urged me not to worry about it. It was worth it to her, she said, to help me in a way that would last a lifetime.

"Fixing my teeth" permanently involved the surgical implantation of two metal rods that fake teeth could be inserted onto. It was expensive and scary, but I made appointments to get quotes to my nana within a week, worried that someone would talk her out of helping me if it took too long. My initial visit to the periodontist made clear that the procedure was going to be even more complicated than we originally thought. The spacing in my teeth didn't leave enough room to insert the metal rods. There was no way around it. A visit to an orthodontist added eight months of braces and thousands of additional dollars onto the estimate, which my nana agreed to immediately. But it meant I had to spend eight months in braces.

The braces weren't that bad. It was my second time having them, so I already knew all the little tricks to keep them clean, all the things I couldn't eat, how to adapt my smile so that my lips didn't get caught in the metal. I was an old pro.

Since my dad and I didn't speak that often, I thought it would be easy to avoid him for a few months, to give myself space until I sorted through my feelings. But my silence and short noncommittal replies to his texts and emails seemed to provoke him, and suddenly our relationship was an urgent priority for him.

He started calling and emailing almost every day, bewildered by my cruelty, alternately angry and sad that I was being so immature and self-righteous. I stopped answering the calls and ignored most of the emails. In the few responses I sent, I asked him to stop contacting me for a little while, told him that I needed time to think. He ignored every request.

"Do you think I should just stop talking to him completely?" I asked Ian.

Ian and I had recently moved in together. I was sitting on our bed in our tiny bedroom in the back of our apartment. Our mattress sat on a bulky elevated frame that Ian had built to increase our storage space. We were using the space under our bed to store our moldy "guest" mattress, some bags of unwanted clothes, and a table saw. I complained about the height of the bed, as it was a good five feet off the ground and difficult for me to climb onto, but I felt proud that Ian had made something so large and practical, and I liked that the height allowed the bed to be pushed right up against the glass of the bedroom window. Even that day in late winter, I felt warm and summery from my perch on our elevated bed.

"I can't answer that," Ian said. "It's a very complicated situation. And I've never met him. I have no idea what he's thinking."

It was not what I wanted to hear. I wanted Ian to say that I was doing what was right for me in this moment. That there was no way for me to be wrong about my feelings. I wanted a complete and unquestioning agreement with my narrative. Actually, that wasn't at all what I wanted. I wanted a nuanced and sincere perspective unbiased by fear or cowardice, which was exactly what Ian had offered.

I sent one more email, explaining in the clearest way I could that I wasn't going to respond anymore and that I needed him to leave me alone for a while.

It was a pretty run-of-the-mill unexpected death. My nana hadn't been sick, but had never been healthy. She had a heart attack, her second one in ten years, alone in her bedroom one night, and one of my aunts found her body the next morning, stiff and appearing to be scared, an image I would prefer not to hold on to for the rest of my life, but I guess whatever.

I was in Ian's car a hundred miles away, already having a bad morning because I'd gotten an email letting me know that I didn't get a job I was really hoping to get, and was running late for the job I still had.

The minute I found out, I became jealous of my former self, the self from just a few seconds prior, for getting to feel bad about something as trivial as a job-related email. Then I got mad at myself for wasting my thoughts by creating unnecessary nostalgia around a negative feeling when I could be productively mourning. Then I got mad at myself for continuing to let my mind focus on itself, to keep wandering away from my nana, who was now dead. *Dead*, I thought. *DEAD. Do you get it?* My mind couldn't seem to comprehend the word.

Not long after I hung up with my mom, I realized I was wearing braces that I couldn't finish paying for, and that the braces were pointless anyway because I couldn't possibly pay for the actual implants that the braces were preparing my mouth for.

I also realized that I had left some important work papers at home, so I called my boss and explained, while sobbing, that I was on my way but that I needed to go back to get the paperwork I'd forgotten and that I'd be a half an hour late and that my nana had just died.

"Don't come to work, Chelsea," my boss said. "Please, take a couple days off."

I didn't know what to do. I wasn't ready to go see my family, but I didn't want to stay home either. I wanted the day to pass without my having to decide what to do with it. I wanted my inner self to disappear and leave just the shell of me, unable to have thoughts or know what my thoughts were or to feel disappointed by the emotional immaturity of my thoughts.

Ian thought we should go thrifting.

"Maybe you'll find something that will remind you of her," he said.

I thought it was a dumb idea, but I agreed because I hated thrifting and I figured it would be a good setting for my misery.

We drove to thrift stores in our area, got hot tea at Starbucks, and talked about little unemotional things. How to shine boots properly. Ian's fourth-grade teacher. The order of the zodiac. I remained distracted and emotionless, except for some surges of love and pride toward Ian for his aptitude in taking care of me. I found nothing that reminded me of my nana at any of the stores, although at the end of the day I did go into Safeway to buy a giant Mr. Goodbar, the kind she always kept hidden in her dresser.

There would be no funeral. That was obvious fairly soon. No one was planning one. Her body sat in a funeral home for five days while her seven children collectively refused to discuss what to do with it.

The five sisters, my nana's daughters, were suddenly on very bad terms. One would only talk to two of the others, who wouldn't talk to each other, though one of those sisters would talk to one of the other sisters, who wanted to talk to three of the sisters, but none of those sisters wanted to talk to her, so she left drunken messages on all their voice mails. There was one who didn't talk to anyone, as far as I knew, and, lastly, my mom, the fifth sister, who would only consistently talk to one sister, but would sometimes take calls from any of the other sisters but be mad about it. The two brothers didn't talk to any of the sisters but possibly talked to each other, and one would sometimes mail long, angry, handwritten letters to each of the sisters. I didn't think this was any of my business until my aunts started blocking me on Facebook. I guess they didn't want me to read their belligerent rants to and about one another.

And then, one by one, my cousins blocked me as well.

My nana and papa had done a pretty good job of fucking up each of their children in a special way that was completely unrelatable to any of the unique ways in which any of their siblings were fucked-up. But my cousins and I had always seemed to be fucked-up in a similar way. We each had the burden of trying to love our parent in a way that would make up for the love they'd missed out on as children. We were each our parent's one chance at unconditional love. But my cousins and I couldn't bond over this, because bonding over it would mean talking about it, which would mean betraying our parents, which would damage the unconditional love we were responsible for giving them.

The fact that my cousin Alana blocked me was especially hurtful. She was four years younger than I was. We had lived together at various times when we were younger and saw each other weekly, if not daily, throughout our childhood and adolescence. She had always felt like a second sister to me, a sister I didn't completely get along with and who was always around, which felt like just what a sister close to my age should be.

I texted her, and she didn't respond. I texted her again, and she didn't respond.

My silence seemed to provoke my dad more than my short emails did.

Sometimes the messages he left would be sweet and sad, just a simple "I miss you," and I would consider writing back. But almost immediately after the nice ones he would send mean, angry messages about what a horrible person I was, how heartless I was for the way I was treating him, and it would remind me why I had stopped talking to him.

I blocked his email address and phone number. He made new email accounts to email me from, like YourSisterMissesYou@gmail.com or StopBeingInsaneChelsea@hotmail.com. I blocked them all.

He had his three-year-old daughter leave me voice mails, saying things like "Chelsea, why don't you want to see me, it makes me sad," his voice softly prompting her in the background.

"Your sister is going to call you in five minutes," he would text from some unknown number. When I didn't pick up the phone five minutes later, I would get a series of angry texts about my "responsibility" to my "sister"—a word that was technically accurate but that I had a hard time applying to this child, whose family didn't feel like my family.

"She's going to call again in five minutes," he would text. "Please pick up this time."

And when I didn't pick up: "Stop playing games."

I had gotten a new job at a web design company, and part of my job was to write blog entries for a fairy-themed website the company managed. I was getting paid more than I ever had in my life, and was making payments toward my braces and saving for the implants.

I would see my dad's dozens of calls and messages all at once when I looked at my phone at the end of the day, his emotional roller coaster playing out while I had been obliviously writing a blog post about the fantastical myths and legends of England. The disconnect between our realities was incredible to me. It was amazing how angry I could make someone simply by being at work during working hours, how "childish" and "attention-seeking" I was being as I wrote about changelings at a wage that allowed me to pay for the dental implants I'd been needing for ten years.

My dad's child's mom, Rozanna, called me half a dozen times, sometimes with seemingly genuine requests that I communicate with their three-year-old, and sometimes with resentment and frustration in her voice. Feeling guilty about her child being manipulated into feeling unloved by me, I called Rozanna and explained my feelings.

Rozanna sounded rational and levelheaded during our conversation, and I was proud of myself for calling and talking to her. I remembered how much I had liked her. She agreed that the fact that my dad was coaching their child to call me was shameful and wrong, but tried to convince me that my bad relationship with him didn't need to interfere with my potential relationships with the two of them. I agreed to consider visiting them, and she agreed to keep quiet about any future plans to do so.

The next day I received several angry messages from my dad telling me not to even think about talking to or seeing his daughter without his supervision, that it would be traumatizing for her to see me without him around.

The situation, strange and opaque to begin with, had turned into something entirely unrecognizable. It had been uncomfortable to begin with for me to purposefully refrain from communicating my feelings. I loved communicating my feelings and believed that honesty was the solution to pretty much every interpersonal problem. But talking seemed to make things worse between me and my dad. I had asked for space to figure out a new way to approach our problems, and my request wasn't even heard.

Even though I wanted the harassment from my dad to end, I didn't change my phone number, in case Alana wanted to reach me. I kept wanting to text her, to figure out what had happened, what had changed so drastically between us that she couldn't respond to a text.

I also couldn't help but feel sympathy for her situation. My dad's behavior towards me when I tried to distance myself from him vindicated my decision to allow the distance between Alana and me to grow. She had made it clear that she didn't want to talk to me. The kind thing to do was wait for her to come back around. I waited for her to text me, wondering if she ever would.

"She's turning twenty-two today," I said.

The next year I said, "She's turning twenty-three."

I had flubbed both situations. I was doing a horrible job at being rejected and possibly an even worse job rejecting someone. I had tried to be accepting of Alana's unexplained absence and it hadn't changed her mind about me. I tried to give myself space from my dad as delicately as I could, explaining things to him as best as I could for as long as I could stand, and he'd ignored every single thing I asked of him. It had all gone completely wrong.

If it were anyone else harassing me, so persistently and for so long, I think I would have handled things differently. I would have been better able to ignore it, or to ask somebody to help me make it stop, or to give his name and photo to my friends and employers so they would know I was being targeted by someone unstable. I wouldn't have been so fearful that people would judge me based on the quality of my relationship with my dad.

This realization made me angry with myself. It proved that my dad meant something to me. That, despite his not having any of the qualifications I considered necessary for him to be regarded as family (which could be as little as standing around in the same rooms every few years), biology had undermined my qualification system and made me kind of care. And it was the kind-of caring that hurt. Each new message from him brought a pang of guilt and dealt a blow to my desire not to give a fuck. Each voice mail from his baby was a chance for me to remind myself that I was okay with being the type of person who is an asshole to babies.

I printed out restraining order paperwork from the internet and tried to understand my options. I was pretty sure I had to file for a domestic violence restraining order, since we were related. But the phrase "domestic violence" made me feel overdramatic. He had never been violent toward me. I didn't fear for my life or my physical well-being. This was a simple case of incessant, unwanted communication from an estranged parent. Why wasn't there a box for that? I filled out the paperwork and printed copies of his emails, but I never sent them in. Would I really have the guts to appear in court, as was required, and tell a judge I was charging my dad with domestic violence because I didn't want him to talk to me? That I just never wanted to ever read another email that demanded I talk to some little girl I didn't want to talk to? Wouldn't that undermine victims of physical domestic violence? Wouldn't I tell someone else in my situation to just suck it up and ignore it?

Why couldn't I just ignore it?

I threw my restraining order papers at the wall and cried.

Maybe I was making things harder on myself. Maybe I should just talk to him one more time. Maybe he would be satiated if I called and talked for a few minutes every once in a while for the rest of my life. Wouldn't that be better than all this?

I thought about my mom. She must have felt so helpless and

betrayed and alone when my dad had disappeared and she became a single parent at seventeen. But despite a period of depression when he left, her descriptions of her pregnancy and my babyhood are filled with happy adjectives. At some point, she told me, all her heartbreak over my dad turned into loving devotion to me. I was not a reminder of love lost, but a symbol of how much love she was capable of feeling, of the possibility that still existed of finding someone worthy to love.

She could have asked his friends where he was, but she didn't. She could have pursued child support, but she didn't. She could have showed up at his father's house and demanded someone be responsible for my dad's poor choices, but she didn't. She accepted his decision. She left him alone.

My dad's dad called me. My grandfather. This was a man I had spoken to once before, briefly. A man who had lived within miles of me my entire life, and who hadn't once tried to see me.

In this first-ever phone call to me, he left me a voice mail lecture about how important it was for me to see my dad's child, how it was my responsibility to be a good sister to her.

I finally changed my phone number.

My dad continued to send me emails from a variety of new email addresses. They were mostly "nice" emails: "Thinking about you. Call me." Or "I love you. I miss you. Hope you're doing well." But the fact that they were "nice" didn't change the fact that they were unwanted. They were almost more unbearable than the fucked-up messages, because it was as if he'd never heard a word I had said. He wasn't arguing with me anymore. He was simply ignoring what I had said and what he had been doing to me for months and acting as if nothing had ever been wrong.

He purchased things from my Etsy store, where I could not block him. At first I sent him the items he bought, with a fake return address (in an attempt to be a responsible small-business owner). Then

I sent the items he bought and included a letter telling him that if he ever truly hoped to talk to me in the future, then he needed to respect my request for space and that I would contact him if I ever wanted to talk (in an attempt to be civil, but firm and direct). Sometimes I refunded his purchases and didn't send them (in an attempt to be ethical but nonparticipatory), and sometimes I kept his money, didn't say anything, and never sent the items he bought (in an attempt to financially discourage him from continuing to buy things from me). I had to stop using my real return address on all outgoing packages, as I never knew if he was placing orders under a pseudonym.

He left comments on comics I published online. I emailed the publisher to ask to have the comments removed, and kept an eye on my postings after that.

He emailed random tertiary friends of mine he had never met, asking for their help getting in touch with me. I apologized to my friends, explaining and defending my choices to people who shouldn't have been involved at all.

He sent me an email that said that if I didn't respond he would come to Oakland and hunt me down.

The phrase "hunt you down" sounded violent, and suggested to me that he was not in control of his emotions. But it also seemed so disconnected from reality, so confused and sad, so powerless. And, actually, I realized, he was mostly powerless. What could he really do, even if he did "hunt me down"? Make me talk to him? Make me like him? Change his personality? Change mine? Change our history?

All at once I felt very strong. Between his long absence and his clumsy return, the decision of whether he was going to be in my life had not been mine to make. But now, it was clear, it *was* mine, regardless of whether he chose to accept it. I didn't have to like him, and I didn't have to talk to him. He could spend all the energy he wanted trying to change those facts, but they were my choices to make. And they always would be.

I've come to think of all my past selves as if they are my daughters.

I want to stand up for them, to make sure that even when they were being very bad they were still loved and understood, even if only by their future self.

I've thought a lot about the particular past self who promised never to write about her dad, to never give him the satisfaction of knowing he had an effect on me. I know how angry and unlovable that past self felt at the time, and wonder if my writing about him now, against her wishes, would feel to her like yet another selfish adult disregarding her feelings in favor of her own interests.

And though I'm comforted by the fact that this past self seemed to know it was always her story to tell or to not tell, I have to admit that what she didn't yet know is that I never keep promises to myself. Promising myself I'll do something is basically a dare to all future selves to do the opposite. It's actually pretty infuriating.

ACKNOWLEDGMENTS

Thank you, Yuka Igarashi, Monika Woods, Ian Amberson, Elizabeth Ellen, Wah-Ming Chang, Chloe Caldwell, and Stephanie Georgopulos. Also Mom, River, and Kylie.